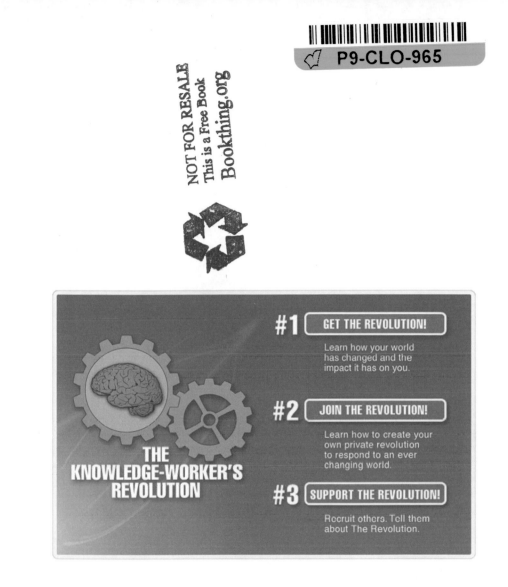

Welcome to Step #2 in the Knowledge Worker's Revolution. If you haven't gotten the revolution yet (Step #1), go to *www.whatsyourgenius.com* to get your free copy of the *Knowledge Worker's Manifesto.*

What's Your Genius?

What's Your Genius?

How the Best THINK for Success in the New Economy

JAY NIBLICK

www.whatsyourgenius.com
whatsyourgenius@gmail.com

Printed in the United States of America.

First Publication: June 15th, 2009

ISBN-10# (0-615-28376-4)
ISBN-13# (978-0-615-28376-0)

"Stop trying to put in what God left out and instead, work with what He put in."

— *Dr. Robert S. Hartman*

Endorsements

"*What's Your Genius* will help you discover your natural talents and reach your peak level of performance—effortlessly! Jay does a great job of helping you learn the secrets of who you are and how you think, so you can create your own private revolution and unleash your greatest potential today. Get ready to evolve."
~ DR. MARSHALL GOLDSMITH, AUTHOR OF *NEW YORK TIMES* BESTSELLING, *WHAT GOT YOU HERE WON'T GET YOU THERE.*

"Jay Niblick's *What's Your Genius* is an absolute must read. This book is more than an inspirational guide; it will transform the way you perceive abilities and limitations, revealing an entirely new scope of life options which are in complete alignment with your core motivations. Simply put, if you read one personal development book this year this should be it."
~ DR. IVAN MISNER, *NEW YORK TIMES* BESTSELLING AUTHOR AND FOUNDER OF BNI

"I figured that if Jay was good enough to advise Tony Robbins, he was good enough for me, so I immediately dove in and began discovering the secrets to achieving my own private revolution. I found Jay's work extremely revealing, insightful and most importantly effective. The lessons in *What's Your Genius* have changed my life forever. Thanks Jay!"
~ TIMOTHY A. MCGINTY, CO-AUTHOR OF *WAKE UP...LIVE THE LIFE YOU LOVE*

"This book is awesome—really awesome. Easily in the same league as *The Five Patterns of Extraordinary Careers*, and Covey's *7 Habits*. When it comes to your journey toward greater success and happiness, *What's Your Genius* is a serious tailwind."
~ MICHAEL LORELLI, FORMER PRESIDENT PEPSICO & PIZZA HUT

"*What's Your Genius* gives you permission to be confident in your God-given talents. Based on years of insightful research, there is wisdom in this book that will help you to recognize the value of your talents and give you confidence to employ them fully. Positive thinking and purposeful action are at the core of its universal message, and it is a book that will open your mind and enlarge your spirit."

~ GARRY TITTERTON, AUTHOR OF *BRAND STORMING*

"As a coach and a person that is passionate about assisting people to reach their highest potential and play their biggest game in life, I found *What's Your Genius* to provide a brilliant and insightful view on determining what drives us. With some great practical tools based firmly in science this book provides a solid method on how to identify where our Genius resides and unleash it."

~ GAVIN FRIEDMAN, CORPORATE & EXECUTIVE COACH

"*What's Your Genius* is the logical and practical application in determining your natural talents. The first step is understanding what your strengths are and then focusing on those strengths in what you do in your life. Jay definitely helps you learn to stop following the crowd and become authentic!"

~ HEATHER WILLIAMSON PhD., PROFESSOR OF SOCIAL PSYCHOLOGY, VIRGINIA COMMONWEALTH UNIVERSITY

"*What's Your Genius* is a fascinating journey into the real reasons behind individual peak performance. Jay shares some powerful and non-conventional lessons learned from some of the most successful people in the world. If you aren't sure where to go, how to get there or are feeling blocked in getting to the next level of performance—you need this book."

~ DR. TONY ALESSANDRA, AUTHOR OF *SECRETS OF TEN GREAT GENIUSES*

"*What's Your Genius* works on a number of levels. Whether it is through Jay's anecdotes, or the comments from other management luminaries or the wealth of research to support Jay's proposition—where the book stands out is in the way that you are taken on the path to enlightenment and self-development. This is not just a book; it is a real process that engages you for the longer term. For the organizations of the world the implications are that they will need to realign their traditional views of people and performance if they are to tap into the genius of their employees."

~ GRAHAM HACKETT, SENIOR MANAGER, BAE SYSTEMS UK

To Melanie, whose Genius has "moved" so many, and to Zach, Baker and Joseph, whose Genius remains untapped and infinite.

Just Do You!

Contents

FOREWORD

During these changing and turbulent times, what is the single biggest factor in shaping the quality of our lives? What affects our ability to not only survive, but also thrive? What are the forces that determine whether we face failure or sustain success?

The truth is these are uncertain times—in 2008, according to the Federal Bureau of Labor Statistics there were 43% more people laid off than in 2007. This year, major companies such as IBM have fired 1400 people in the month of January alone. The times are uncertain, but while we have minimum control in being able to change the external environment, we do have maximum power in being able to shift our internal environment—being able to control not only what a situation means to us, but also how we show up. To get the best out of the worst times, we need to demand the best from ourselves—we need to perform at our peak level.

After having the privilege of spending thirty years serving over three million people from over 100 different countries, I know that there are certain patterns that create success and other patterns that breed failure. I've had the pleasure of working with elite, peak performers in business, politics, entertainment and sports such as legendary basketball Coach John Wooden, who won a record ten NCAA championships in twelve years. Coach Wooden's philosophy was simple: "Don't let what you cannot do interfere with what you can do." To him, it was not about winning or losing, it was about getting the best out of his players' ability, allowing them to focus on their strengths and not their weaknesses. If we adopted a similar focus, we would not only set ourselves up to win in these trying times, but we would be fulfilled in the process. I believe that *success without fulfillment is failure.*

In fact, the definition of success is being able to achieve your goals and be fulfilled in the process. The secret to achieving and being fulfilled is having the courage to go beyond the skills you've learned and discover the gifts that you were born to give and to employ them daily. So many people settle and adapt to the work or career they've chosen or fallen into. They might even say, "Well, obviously I've got to enjoy my work. I picked it, didn't I?" While that may be true, the question is: Did you pick it consciously, knowing what your gifts are, knowing what's inside of you that is most powerful? Again, I'm not referring to the part of you that's been educated and trained. We can all train ourselves to do just about anything. This is about the part of you that you were born to use, to contribute, and to serve at a higher level.

Most people pick their work or career unconsciously, based upon conditioning, proximity or expectation—based on reasons that were not completely their own. When that happens, it increases the gap between achieving a depth of success and living a life of meaning and "just getting by." As long as that gap remains—as long as they're trying to do something they're not thrilled about or something that isn't part of their nature—they might achieve in the short-term, but they will never succeed in the long-term.

It's essential for today's employers to recognize and cultivate their employees' talents and gifts if they want to retain them and remain viable in the marketplace. And it's critical for employees to understand what really motivates them in order to be able to communicate these needs to their employers and generate opportunities for win-win situations—where they are committed to peak performance and feel like there's principle and enjoyment in what they do; where business owners and managers are nurturing and efficiently supporting their staff; and companies are reaping the benefits of cooperation and optimal productivity.

Jay Niblick's in-depth, comprehensive study *What's Your Genius* represents a truly ground-breaking approach toward innovating how we think of our careers, our life's purpose, and ourselves. Niblick has taken on the tremendous responsibility of transforming cultural attitudes about work and achievement that have been in place for more than a century, while simplifying the exhaustive academic legwork that legitimizes the importance of individual authenticity.

He introduces easily-implementable strategies for not only attaining that sense of real accomplishment we all long for in life, but also a truly profound understanding of who we really are at our core. With these imperative components in place, finding fulfillment in what we do does not have to be reserved for the lucky few. With a few minor (and in some cases, major) adjustments to our perceptions, what people want most out of themselves and this key aspect of life is readily available.

Whether you're pursuing your dreams as an entrepreneur or exploring other career options, being authentic and actively appreciating what you're really capable of is going to be one of the most important forms of social and economic capital in the coming years.

It will make the difference between mediocrity and excellence; the difference between "just getting by" and really thriving instead. It's the psychological and emotional edge that will help us create better lives not only for ourselves, but also for everyone that we influence in our global community. With increasing economic pressure, now more than ever, is the time to extract the best out of yourself and to use that gift to touch the lives of others.

Jay Niblick's *What's Your Genius?* will give you the tools to utilize your strengths to reap higher returns and the success that, as Coach Wooden puts it, "comes from knowing that you did your best to become the best that you are capable of becoming."

— Anthony Robbins
May 2009

INTRODUCTION

Did you ever have that one class in school where no matter how hard you tried you just never seemed to get it? No matter how hard you studied, no matter how hard you worked, results just never seemed to come easily, if at all. Even if you did do well, was it always a struggle? If you're like most people, there was also another class where the exact opposite was true and things just came to you almost effortlessly. The whole concept just made sense, and you achieved greater success more naturally with less effort.

One reason for this is that each of us has certain innate talents for thinking and making decisions. These natural thinking talents allow us to see some things very clearly while filtering out others almost completely. For example, some people naturally see the big picture very easily (the talent for strategic thinking) or intuitively understand how various parts work together (the talent for integrative ability), while for others understanding complex problems is like second nature (the problem-solving talent).

Our thinking talents and decision-making styles comprise the very core of who we are. They make us the unique individuals that we see in the mirror each morning, and they hold the greatest potential for delivering our greatest levels of performance and success.

The most recent scientific evidence would argue that these decision-making styles are engrained in who we are by both our genetics and early life experiences. As a result, while these thinking talents may change and develop slightly over the course of our lives, these are not things that you can develop through training exercises or sheer effort in adulthood. If your job (or class) depends heavily on a thinking talent that you don't possess, or if it doesn't align well with what thinking talents you do possess, you are in trouble. You will always be that student sitting in the difficult class, working harder than anyone else yet still achieving less success.

Conventional wisdom, however, would argue that you should do just that. The traditional view of self-improvement says that it is good to place yourself in that difficult class, to become well rounded in a wide variety of areas and to identify your weaknesses so you can *fix* them and turn them into strengths. Unfortunately, conventional wisdom, which this book will challenge, is based on time-honored principles, and the problem with such principles is that they can become subject to less and less consideration over time. Eventually, such "wisdom" becomes such a part of the norm that it fails to be questioned at all, becoming accepted without question—even when it is wrong.

What's Your Genius is the result of seven years of research into what drives individual performance and excellence. As part of this research, we looked at over 197,000 people—including some of the most successful people in a wide variety of fields—to see if we could identify common factors present among the top performers. The study separated performance into five levels with the fifth level being the peak of performance or what we called "Genius." So this isn't a book about how to increase your intelligence; it's a book about how to help anyone reach peak levels of performance by being true to their own natural thinking talents—their own "best way" (i.e. their genius).

What the study revealed is that the most successful people don't follow conventional wisdom. They understand that their natural talents are fixed and therefore they don't spend their lives trying in vain to change their natural thinking talents. They understand that they are who they are, and instead of wasting vast amounts of energy trying to become something they are not, they invest that energy in trying to better apply the natural talents they already possess. To quote an expert in the field, Dr. Robert Hartman, today's best performers, "stop trying to put in what God left out and instead work with what He put in."

The message isn't that you don't have to work hard to be successful. It isn't that you shouldn't continually attempt to expand and grow either. Learning what your natural thinking talents are, and learning how to utilize them for maximum effect is plenty hard enough. The message of this book is that there is a difference between working hard in the dark and working hard in the light—the full light of awareness for what and who you are and how best to leverage that for optimal success.

Dr. Marshall Goldsmith, one of the Geniuses interviewed in the research, says that when it comes to continuing to develop and refine himself, "I constantly try to refine the strengths I have, but that doesn't mean I try to develop things I don't already have. One danger in the message of only focusing on strengths is that people may perceive this to mean that they don't have to improve at all. Rather, within their natural talents they must always improve. The key is to find a role that depends primarily on what you do well, then continue to get even better at it through practice, awareness, acquired knowledge and experience." Marshall goes on to say, "There are a whole lot of things I stink at. I just make sure I don't have to do them to be successful."

To succeed today you must find your own best way to do things, because when we really know ourselves, when we are completely authentic to our natural thinking talents, when we create goals and objectives that feed off those talents, an almost mystical energy seems to show up in what we are doing. The stars seem to align, and, as Basil King put it, "mighty forces come to our aid."

In the end it's not about fixing who we are, it is about *trusting* who we are and letting our natural talents do their thing. In that moment—where all of our talents are optimally aligned with what we are doing—anyone really can become a genius.

Some of the successful people studied who helped teach us this truth include:

- Anthony Robbins—Personal Life Coach and Peak Performance expert;
- Dan Lyons—CEO of Team Concepts Inc., seven-time National Team member, World Champion and Olympian in rowing;
- Frances Hesselbein—Founding Director of the Peter F. Drucker Foundation and former CEO of Girl Scouts of America;
- Laurence Higgins, M.D.—Chief of Sports Medicine and Shoulder at Harvard;
- Dr. Marshall Goldsmith—*NY Times* best-selling business author & executive coach to Fortune 500 CEOs;
- Michael Lorelli—former Chief Marketing Officer and President of PepsiCo East and Pizza Hut International;
- Mickey Rogers—World Authority Demolitions Expert;
- Randy Haykin—Founding Vice President Sales/ Marketing Yahoo Inc.; and
- Rosemary Hygate—Executive Assistant to the stars

How to Use This Book

Sir Frances Bacon once said, "Knowledge is power." Unfortunately, he was only half correct, because only *applied* knowledge is power; otherwise it remains only potential power. While this book will indeed give you new knowledge about yourself and your natural thinking talents, the great challenge is not to understand the practice of being successful, it is learning how to practice that understanding.

As Benjamin Franklin once said, "Tell me and I will forget, show me and I might remember, involve me and I will understand." Throughout this book you will be given a lot of new knowledge, but to help you really understand that knowledge, you will also be asked to complete certain activities. These are called Genius Action Steps, and they reside in an online suite of tools developed specifically for this book. You now have free access to all of these tools.

Go to: *www.whatsyourgenius.com/workbook* to create your own free account and access your private workbook. It only takes a few seconds, the system is a secure, password-encrypted site, and you will be the only one who has access to it.

Throughout the book whenever you see the symbol below you will know it is time to go to your WYG online workbook to complete a short exercise or activity to help you apply some new bit of knowledge.

CHAPTER 1

The Problem

I could see the frustration in her face, and I could hear it in her voice. As I sat there listening to Lina describe her current level of satisfaction with her life, her job and her success, it was glaringly apparent that she was tired, frustrated and just plain spent from working harder than she thought she should have to, only to achieve less than she wanted to. She didn't feel her current job was allowing her to reach her full potential.

Lina and I were sitting in a coffee bar in downtown Zurich, Switzerland where earlier that day I had given a lecture to a group of executives and entrepreneurs on the key drivers of individual performance and excellence. At the end of the lecture I asked the simple question, "How many of you feel satisfied with your current level of personal performance and believe that your role allows you to reach your fullest potential?" The show of hands throughout the room might have represented half of the attendees at best—a room containing over 300 individuals. And there I stood, yet again, staring out into a room full of people with both hands on their laps, looking around somewhat sheepishly, not very excited about their inability to raise their hands up high.

I say "yet again" because this wasn't the first time I had asked this question. I've asked it all over the world, and the response is pretty much the same no matter where I go—from Istanbul to Sydney, New York to Hong Kong, Johannesburg to Zurich. And every time I've asked that relatively simple question (a question one would hope is not asking too much), at best 50% of the crowd raises their hands while the rest remain timidly still, indicating more to themselves than anyone else that when they really think about it, they do not feel truly fulfilled in their work or fully satisfied with their own performance and success.

In talking more closely with many of these people, I find that they:

- Feel frustrated and unfulfilled;
- Feel that they put in more effort than they get out in results;
- Feel they have lots of unrealized potential;
- Are dissatisfied with their performance and success; and
- Know they can be happier and more passionate.

Simply put, they don't feel their current roles allow them to maximize their full potential.

Perhaps even scarier than the percentages is the realization of whom I am talking to in these presentations. I typically present only to executives and entrepreneurs, so if the leaders of the world's organizations aren't fully satisfied and passionate about what they do, what does that mean for the organizations and people they lead?

~ I feel like I put in more than I get out. ~

For Lina, the vice president of Human Resources at a mid-sized retail company, one of the most telling indicators of her lack of fulfillment and satisfaction came in her acknowledgment that more weeks than not, she looked forward to the weekends but dreaded Mondays. Lina had a first-class case of the "golden handcuffs." As the primary breadwinner for her family, and with three young children at home and a husband out of work, she needed the financial rewards her job provided. Unfortunately those were some of the only rewards it provided. Outside of providing her with the money she needed and some dear friends, Lina's job left her constantly battling to achieve the results and success she wanted. In her own words, she didn't feel that her job allowed her to be "true" to herself. This feeling of being "untrue," it turns out, is a constant theme among far too many unhappy people around the world.

Lina was cuffed to a job that she couldn't afford to leave, financially, but couldn't afford to stay in emotionally either. As a result, her dissatisfaction was up and her passion and results were down—way down.

Lina isn't alone. In my work as a business consultant and coach, I have met too many people who feel unfulfilled in their roles and are frustrated with the lack of performance and success they achieve. All too often I meet people who work to live instead of the other way around. I'm not alone in these observations.

A recent Harris poll[1] of 23,000 individuals revealed that only half were satisfied with the work they had accomplished by the end of the week. It's so common for people not to be fully in love with what they do that we've even developed cliché's like: Mental Health Days, the Monday morning blues, Hump day and TGIF.

How many times have you heard someone make the following kind of statement:

- "I can't wait for retirement";
- "Tell me again why I'm here";
- "I never seem to get ahead";
- "I'm just going through the paces, I'm bored"; or
- "Something's missing"?

How many times have you made a similar statement? How fulfilled are you in your current role? Do you feel like you are free to use all of your natural talents and potential in the work you do every day? If you found yourself in one of my lectures, would you raise your hand?

---

[1] For more information about the Harris Poll, visit *www.harrisinteractive.com*.

Over the past ten years, I've seen so many people suffering from the same kinds of issues that eventually I gave it a name. Now I just refer to it as *The Problem*. The formal definition of The Problem is "a growing trend of people who feel unfulfilled in their roles and dissatisfied and frustrated with results or success."

Regardless of the level of performance, any individual who feels unable to improve for long enough will start to become uninspired, impassionate and dissatisfied with their performance. They will eventually begin to suffer from The Problem.

Today, too many people are suffering from The Problem. And, given the increasing frequency and globalization of this problem, I decided to try to find out what was behind it in the first place. I wanted to better understand the differences between those who did and did not suffer from The Problem. Why did some, despite great effort, constantly struggle to achieve moderate levels of performance and success, while others achieved significantly more success much more frequently and with less effort and frustration?

I knew I had to find some answers. Otherwise, more Linas of the world would be dreading Mondays, and more people would be leaving their hands on their laps and their true potential unrealized.

And so was born the Genius Project.

~ The Problem is an epidemic of people who feel frustrated and dissatisfied with their own performance and success. ~

R | **Chapter 1 Review**

- "The Problem" is an epidemic of people that feel unfulfilled, dissatisfied and frustrated with their performance.

CG | **Chapter 1 Gut Check**

How fulfilled are you? Many times people have a passionate reason for getting into a line of work, but then something happens. Things get added. You take on new roles and new responsibilities, and before you know it you are off course. These new additions are like tiny steps, each one taking them just a little bit further away from their original objective. Because these steps are so tiny, and because they are often driven by positive desires, they are easy to miss. But they add up, and the next thing you know you are way off course. In the military, we had a term for getting off-course like this. We called it "Mission Creep."

Have you gotten off course? Has your original objective grown into something you don't recognize or like anymore? When you stop to look up, are you where you thought you would be, or wanted to be, five years ago?

How far have you crept from where you intended to be? (circle one)

Very far away 1 2 3 4 5 *Right where I want to be*

To help you determine how significant The Problem may or may not be for you, please go online now and take the first Genius Action Step. If you haven't set up your account, please do that first, then you can complete this short exercise to help you assess objectively just how satisfied you are with your own level of performance and how fulfilled you feel in your roles.

G | **Genius Action Step 1:** Please log into your WYG Online workbook and complete the Problem Pre-Assessment.

"The Problem" Self-assessment results

Now that you have completed Genius Action Step #1, let's go over what the results mean. This self-assessment has eight categories designed to help create a comprehensive overview of your level of satisfaction in life. Some of the categories covered are things we have not yet discussed, but it's good that we gather them all at the same time, up front, to get the most objective and unbiased opinion possible. Those categories are:

- Self-awareness—How aware are you of your talents and non-talents?
- Authenticity—How true to those talents are you in your roles and work?
- Level of Performance—At what level do you feel you are performing?
- Self-Direction—How clear is your vision for where you want to go?
- Role Awareness—How well do you understand your roles in life?
- Self-Belief—How much belief do you have in your ability to succeed?
- Effort/Ease—How much effort do you have to put in to get results?
- Levels of Satisfaction—How satisfied are you with your overall success?

Your assessment gives you an overall score for each category. If you scored less than four (4) on the overall score then The Problem is a significant one for you, and the lessons in this book will be significant for you. If you scored less than four in any single category, then that category should become a primary focus in the exercises to come. To that end, I recommend that you print a copy of this self-assessment out so you can refer back to it from time to time throughout the rest of this book.

Simply put, the lower you scored on the Problem Pre-Assessment, the more you probably need this book.

Note: If you know someone whom you think is also suffering from The Problem, you can invite him or her to take the same self-assessment for free. Check out the "share with a friend" button online.

CHAPTER 2

The Genius Project

Michael Lorelli is one of those guys who some might like to hate, and I mean this in the kindest of ways. I'm sure, like all of us, Michael has had his share of failures, but overall he is a guy who has managed to succeed more often than not. You could say it has become a way of life for him. At the age of 18 he earned his private pilot's license in just three weeks. He finished his MBA at NYU in twelve months. He has been the Chief Marketing Officer at PepsiCo, President of PepsiCo East and President of Pizza Hut's international division, finding significant success in each role. He was responsible for the first-ever commercial advertisement on the sails of a boat in the America's Cup race (thanks to Michael we now can barely make out the shape of a boat behind the flurry of advertisements). He was also the first one ever to put a commercial advertisement in a home video (Paramount's smash hit, *Top Gun* in 1987).

Clearly Michael is a guy who gets things done, and in talking with him I found the exact opposite of what I'd heard from Lina. Here was a person who suffered little to no real frustration, outside of the relatively normal amount we all do at least. He didn't feel unfulfilled at all, and he certainly didn't think that he put in more effort than he got out in results. Everything I saw in Lina's face was completely absent from Michael's. All the stress, tension, struggles and frustration to feel satisfied and successful that existed in one were absent in the other. What was it then that was different about the two? Both are very intelligent, well educated, in environments that were conducive to success and superior performance…at least for some.

One difference that jumped out at me was that Michael was quick to say that he has always been *true* to himself. He has always lead from his gut and gone with his natural talents instead of having to depend on his weaknesses. When he has been *true* to his natural talents he has found that success came more naturally, but when he has been *untrue* to himself success has eluded him.

Remember Lina's comments about not feeling that her role allowed her to be true to herself? Michael felt that the exact opposite was the case in his life. This *authenticity* that Michael described is something we found to be common among the most successful people we studied and least common among those who suffered from the problem. It actually turns out to be one of the core findings of the research and central themes of this book.

The Genius Project

The Genius Project was originally only the nickname for the study we started in 2000 called the *Innermetrix Comparative Performance Study* (now you see why we decided to stick with the nickname!). This study spanned seven years, involved 197,000 individuals across twenty-three countries, and was designed to identify any causes that might explain the difference between the best and the rest. In our effort to understand the differences between these two groups, each individual was given a scientifically validated instrument called the Attribute Index[2]. This profile measured each individual's ability in a wide variety of attributes relevant to individual performance. These attributes are naturally occurring talents that people possess based on

---

[2] To receive your own free Genius Profile, visit *www.whatsyourgenius.com*.

how they think and make decisions. The science behind this profile has been rigorously validated, and proven through its use in business for more than fifty years.

We also chose these attributes because we, as a company, had lots of experience with them. This is important when you are trying to understand what these data are telling you. We already had over seventy-five PhDs and 900 certified professional consultants and coaches around the world with the experience and understanding required to accurately administer and interpret the results.[3]

The results of this study are the main underpinnings of this entire book, and the rest of the book will tell you what we found and what you can do to take advantage of this new knowledge to become more successful and satisfied yourself.

What's a Genius?

"Genius is the ability to put into effect what is in your mind."
~ F. SCOTT FITZGERALD

To be able statistically to compare the differences between the most and least successful people, we needed to separate them into categories of performance. We started with a fairly universal set of four levels of performance:

- 1st Level—below average;
- 2nd Level—average;
- 3rd Level—above average; and
- 4th Level—excellent.

Very early on, however, as we started interviewing people and looking at the best performers, we began to see the need for perhaps yet another level of performance. Those who were describing the absolute

---

[3] For corporations interested in learning how to unleash the genius in their organizations, see the resource guide at the back of this book.

best performers were having trouble with the four levels of performance. The interviewees were telling us that these people were better than excellent. You've no doubt seen this yourself. Think of someone who is so damn good at what they do that they are better than "excellent." The word falls short of conveying just how good these people really are.

Time and time again, as we conducted our interviews, the word used to describe these "better than excellent" people was "genius." They would say, "John is so great at seeing the big picture, he is a genius at that," or, "Mary is an absolute genius when it comes to understanding the client's problem."

Because we heard this talk of "better than excellent" so much, we decided to add another level of performance on top of excellent. This became the 5th Level of performance, and because we heard the word genius so many times, that became the nickname for this new level.

The revised rankings then became:

- 1st Level—below average;
- 2nd Level—average;
- 3rd Level—above average;
- 4th Level—excellent; and
- **5th Level—genius.**

When I say "Genius," by the way, I'm not referring to a person's IQ. My use of the word has nothing to do with how intelligent a person is, but everything to do with how well he or she performs. Genius in this sense is descriptive of a person's ability to perform, due to his or her own natural talents.

Someone once asked me, "Not everyone can be a genius right?" My answer to this question was a definitive "yes, everyone can be a genius—they just need to figure out how and at what." I truly believe that anyone can indeed be a genius at something; the trick is to figure out at what. That might be a genius surgeon or genius sales person or architect, but that might also mean a genius auto mechanic or genius server in a restaurant or even a genius janitor. The descriptor "Genius" doesn't have to be used only for high profile or high paid roles. It isn't reserved for celebrities, artists or scientists alone. Somewhere out there is someone doing a job that no one would normally associate with a genius, but any role that exists can be fulfilled at a genius level.

But yes, even geniuses have bad days or weeks or even years. Even the best can't deliver genius-level performance all the time at everything they do. Our lives and our roles are constantly changing. We grow into new duties and responsibilities. We outgrow roles and employers. When such changes occur, even geniuses can struggle with delivering peak performance.

The geniuses I interviewed would be the first to admit that they have had lots of roles in their lives in which they were not able to be geniuses. What differentiates them from non-geniuses, though, is that they realize this fact and don't allow themselves to take up permanent residence in those roles.

Their willingness to try new things, and their ability to recognize that those new things may have been a mistake, are two keys that make them the geniuses they are today.

The Findings

Before we talk about what we did find in the Genius Project, let's look at what we did not find, because that's actually quite important as well. We wondered if the data would reveal certain natural thinking talents that were only present in the most successful and missing in the rest.

After crunching all of that data, what we did *not* find was a single natural thinking talent that showed up in only the most successful.

It turns out that being better at seeing the big picture (the natural talent known as Conceptual Thinking) is not more likely to make *everyone* successful than is being better at seeing the small picture (the natural talent for Attention to Detail). Neither does being better at understanding others (Empathy) have any greater impact on success *across the board* than does being great at doing what you are told to do (Following Directions).

Sure, in some roles a specific set of talents may be more critical to success than others. We see this all the time with our corporate clients, but did not find any thinking talents that correlated with success in every role and job.

For example, possessing the natural talents for understanding and persuading others is crucial in most sales roles, but when you look at non-sales roles those talents may have little impact on success. Yes, some natural talents may indeed be vital in certain roles, perhaps even lots of roles, but not in all roles.

That's right. We failed to find any single natural talent that was the key differentiator between success and failure in *all* cases. While this might sound disappointing at first, it's actually great news!

It's great because were this the case, and had we found talents that must be present in order to succeed, you would pretty much be out of luck if you didn't already possess them. You'd be out of luck because natural talents are hard-wired or engrained in how our minds work, and as such, they can't be developed through learning and effort. If we had found certain talents that were mandatory for success in any role, then only people with those talents would be able to become geniuses. But thankfully that's not what we found.

When I say that we didn't find any *natural* talents, however, that doesn't mean we didn't find any correlations at all among the most successful people. It just means that we didn't find any natural talents that correlated. What we *did* find in the Genius Project were two acquired *skills,* and these two skills were present in all of the successful people, and quite absent in those who suffered from The Problem.

Natural talents come from the way your mind is built, and because of this, they do not change much over the course of your life. Skills, on the other hand, are a form of acquired talent. Skills are the knowledge and experience that you learn throughout your life, and they can be developed. If natural talents are engrained in you early on in life, skills are added later. If natural talents are fixed and something you can't develop through conscious effort, skills are the opposite.

As I said, all of this is great news, because it simply means that, regardless of the natural talents you possess, you can take whatever those talents are and become more successful with them. This means that the playing field is level. Genius performance isn't reserved for just the most intelligent. It isn't just for those who were lucky enough to be born with certain talents. Everyone possesses his or her own unique set of natural talents, so anyone can become a genius at something.

Natural Talents: Are your *innate* ability to do something, your natural endowment or aptitude. The key word here is natural. These talents can be physical, as in Lance Armstrong's remarkable lung capacity (a physical talent due to his anatomy and physiology) or they can be mental as in Anthony Robbins' ability to speak and engage people through words (a mental talent due to his high empathetic ability). The natural talents we are concerned with in this book are only those mental ones we all possess. Natural (mental) talents are patterns of thinking and decision-making that you were either born with or that you developed very early on in life.

Based on your genetics and the way your brain is structured, you are naturally good at seeing certain things, while you may be completely blind to others. Those things you see clearly are your natural talents, whereas those things you do not see clearly are your non-talents. We all have our own unique mix of these two. Your set of natural talents is unique to you. In the entire world, no two people possess the exact same set or level of natural thinking talents.

Acquired Skills: Unlike natural talents, skills are those abilities that we *can* acquire or develop. These are the knowledge and experience we gain throughout life. The person who doesn't possess a natural talent for empathy may, through lots of reading and training, become somewhat competent at being sensitive to needs and emotions of others. The person who isn't naturally good at seeing the big, strategic view may take classes on strategic planning and become somewhat proficient in that area.

The sales person who learns the technical steps of the sale and the features, functions and benefits of the product has a form of acquired skill for selling. The airline pilot who has learned the principles of flight and aerodynamics has an acquired skill for flying. The differences between acquired skills and natural talents, however, are significant, and having one without the other will never deliver 5th-level performance.

The sales person who has acquired knowledge and experience only has one half of the picture. If he doesn't possess the natural talents for being aggressive, persistent or empathetic, then all that acquired talent may be for naught. If he isn't aggressive enough, then he won't apply the necessary steps of the sale when he needs to. If he isn't persistent enough, he is likely not to get past the gatekeeper to talk to the key decision-maker in the first place.

Without the natural talents to support him, all of his skills will not make him a genius at what he does. What success he does achieve will be like the student in that difficult class who struggles to get results. He may get them, but not easily, not passionately, not consistently and not without feeling like he has to put in a lot more effort than what he gets out in results.

I fly a lot, and I'm glad that the pilots who fly me around the world have the skills for knowing how to actually pilot a Boeing 777 from Hartsfield to Heathrow. But I would not want to fly with someone who didn't also have the natural talents for decisiveness, intuitive decision-making and an ability called compartmentalization that the best pilots possess. Being technically proficient is important, but in the moment when the left engine goes out and the pilot has seconds to react, if he lacks the natural talents to go along with his acquired knowledge and skill, I wouldn't want to be on that plane with him.

Every role is different, as is every person who fills it, but the one thing we've learned in this study is that without natural talents, performance will be hindered. Every role, in order to be performed at genius levels, requires that the right natural talent be present. The 5th level of performance is impossible without natural talents.

Now that you understand the difference between natural talents and acquired skills, here are the two skills we discovered in the study. They are called *self-awareness* and *authenticity*.

Acquired Skill #1. Self-Awareness

Self-awareness looks at how aware people are of their own natural thinking talents. For example, does John know he has a great natural talent for strategic thinking that makes him a genius for seeing the big picture and making accurate, long-range plans? How aware is Mary that her greatest natural talent is in empathizing and understanding others? Self-awareness also looks at how well a person understands where he or she does not have a natural talent (i.e. their non-talents). So, while John knows he has a natural talent for strategic thinking, is he also aware that paying attention to details or being empathetic are not two of his strongest talents?

Many people make a common mistake in assuming that self-awareness is automatic. They think, "Surely if you possess some natural talent, you must be aware of it right?" Unfortunately, this is simply not the case. Just because someone has a natural ability for something doesn't ensure that they fully appreciate it. Being self-aware is more than simply thinking, "I could do that." Being self-aware requires a much deeper understanding for the way you think and make decisions and the natural talents you possess as a result.

Being self-aware is being aware of your own true potential, which is a beautiful thing. In F. Scott Fitzgerald's *The Great Gatsby*, Jay Gatsby is described as having, "something gorgeous about him, some heightened sensitivity to the promises of life." When people have high levels of self-awareness, they too seem to hold a heightened sensitivity to all the promise they contain. They know very well what they are and are not good at, and what potential lies within them.

If self-awareness deals with the knowledge you have for your natural talents, then the second acquired skill deals with how you apply those talents. We call this skill *authenticity*.

Acquired Skill #2. Authenticity

Authenticity, at its simplest level, is "being true to you." Being self-aware is only half the picture. Properly applying that knowledge to your life is the other half. Setting goals that capitalize on your natural talents is "being authentic." Finding a job that depends primarily on your natural talents is "being authentic." Working from your strengths is "being authentic."

The opposite of being authentic is being inauthentic. Whether you are aware of your natural thinking talents or not, whenever you fail to properly incorporate them into what you do and how you do it, you are being inauthentic. When you allow yourself to fill a role that requires natural talents that you don't possess (but hope to develop), you are being inauthentic.

Of all the people we studied, the only two things that turned out to be really different between the most successful and the rest were their level of understanding for their natural talents and their ability to act on these talents—to incorporate them into what they do and how they do it.

The message in this study then becomes: the more completely you know your own natural talents (i.e. are self-aware), and the truer you are to those talents (i.e. are authentic), the greater your satisfaction and performance will be.

Figure 1 below demonstrates the simplicity of this concept.

Philosopher G.E. Moore put it as simply as anyone when he said, "Everything is what it is, and not another thing." In other words, we are what we are, and not what we are not. We are our natural talents and our non-talents, and the more aware of these we are—the truer we are to this fact—the better we perform. Trying to be something we are not is fruitless. If your natural talent is not for strategic thinking, then the more your success depends on this ability, the more you are likely to suffer from The Problem.

~ Only when we are what we are, and our roles and objectives are true to that—only then can we reach the 5th level of performance. ~

Figure 1. Authentic Performance Model

A Simple Mistake

The problem, though, is that the vast majority of people assume there is no real difference between talents and skills. They assume that natural talents can be developed through learning, training and hard work. They fail to appreciate just how fixed the neural networks that control these talents really are. Instead, because they fail to differentiate between talents and skills, and because they assume that *both* can be acquired equally, they set about identifying what talents and skills they need for a given role and then start trying to develop them both.

When they do this, they are only halfway successful. They may manage to develop new skills, but they don't develop new talents. They don't change the neural networks that control natural thinking talents. In so doing, they may indeed become one of the most knowledgeable sales people in the company, but they still don't *think* like the great sales people. They become the greatest knowledge expert on the planet for the rules of accounting and the workings of mathematics, but they still don't *think* like the great accountants do. They become the pilot who knows more about the technical manual than the engineer who wrote it, but they still don't meld with the controls and become one with the plane as an extension of their own body, like the great pilots do.

Don't get me wrong. Training and development are vital to success, but by assuming that training and development will develop the natural thinking talents *and* skills they need, many people fail to understand that they are only building up half of the picture. When the other half of the picture isn't there (the natural talents half) they wonder why they continue to struggle. Unfortunately, when people fail to achieve the level of performance they want, the solution is often even more training and knowledge.

People exert a tremendous amount of energy attempting to change themselves in a way that just isn't going to lead to success, when in reality it is the outside world that needs to be changed. That's what geniuses do, they change the world in which their natural talents play.

The Numbers

From a purely statistical perspective, the correlations between self-awareness, authenticity and performance are significant:

- The average level of self-awareness for the 5th-level performers in the study was 89%, compared to 62% for the 4th-level performers, and less than 47% for the 1st- through 3rd-level performers;
- Those who were 5th-level performers had levels of authenticity that were 91% versus levels of authenticity seen in the 4th-level performers of 79% and in the 1st- through 3rd-level performers, who were at or below 63%;
- Correlation between self-awareness and performance was $p = 0.893$;[4] and
- Correlation between authenticity and performance was $p = 0.879$.

These differences make a very compelling argument for becoming more self-aware and authentic. Figure 1a below shows you just how significant the differences are between the five levels of performance studied.

---

[4] A Pearson's Coefficient of Correlation (p) above 0.700 is considered to be significant.

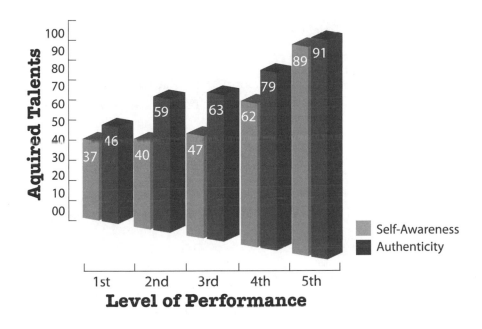

These data show us that there is a direct and positive correlation between the two acquired skills of self-awareness and authenticity and performance. Those who performed at the lower levels also had lower levels of self-awareness and authenticity, but the higher the performance went the greater the level of self-awareness and authenticity became.

| R | **Chapter 2 Review**

Chapter 1:
- "The Problem" is an epidemic of people that feel unfulfilled, dissatisfied and frustrated with their performance.

Chapter 2:
- To find out why, we created the Genius Project, and what we found were two key things:
  - There is no one "Genius Talent"; and
  - Self-Awareness and Authenticity are present in higher levels in the best performers.

| CG | **Chapter 2 Gut Check**

If you look at the times in your life when you have felt the most passionate, the most fulfilled and the most *natural* at what you were doing, these are probably times when you were being authentic. These are also times when I bet you were much more successful with less effort and stress. Please think of a role, or major aspect of a role, that you have filled in the past that you were passionate about and did very well, and then answer the questions below.

What was this role, and which part of it came naturally for you?

_____

_____

How comfortable were you at that time? (circle one)

    Very Uncomfortable 1 2 3 4 5 *Very Comfortable*

How happy were you? (circle one)

    Very Unhappy 1 2 3 4 5 *Very Happy*

How successful were you? (circle one)

Very Unsuccessful   1   2   3   4   5   *Very Successful*

Now think of a role, or major aspect of a role, in which you did not feel this way; where you struggled; where you did not feel passionate about what you were doing, and you did not perform as well as you wanted to. You probably didn't enjoy it, didn't do it well and if you had your druthers, wouldn't do it again. Chances are very good that these were times when you were not being authentic.

In that moment, how were you being inauthentic?

_____

_____

How comfortable were you at that time? (circle one)

Very Uncomfortable   1   2   3   4   5   *Very Comfortable*

How happy were you? (circle one)

Very Unhappy   1   2   3   4   5   *Very Happy*

How successful were you? (circle one)

Very Unsuccessful   1   2   3   4   5   *Very Successful*

This is just a short little exercise to give you a glimpse of what it feels like to be a Genius every day, because Geniuses find ways to make sure almost everything they do feels like the first set of questions. They always strive to be authentic. The question to you is, "Would you rather create a life where you feel like the first scenario all the time, or would you rather continue to experience lots of the second scenario?" As you will see, the choice is yours alone.

CHAPTER 3

The Answer—Two Directions In Life

What Geniuses Do

Geniuses don't make that simple mistake. They don't spend their lives trying to become the A+ student in that difficult class I mentioned in the introduction. They understand they are who they are, so instead of wasting energy trying to become something they are not, they invest it in trying to better apply the natural talents they already possess. In a sense, they stop trying to put in what God left out and instead work with what He put in. This frees up a lot of extra energy. Imagine how much more successful you would be if 100% of your energy was directed toward using your natural talents more effectively.

To illustrate the different perspective that the most successful take, here's a simple visual diagram.

Below are the four universal steps that everyone goes through in any role:

- Step 1—The person accepts a job/role.
- Step 2—They get to know the role better and figure out what it really takes to be successful in it.

- Step 3—Inevitably, they identify gaps between what the job requires and what they can provide (e.g. talents, knowledge, skills, etc.).
- Step 4—They attempt to close the gaps between what is needed and what they possess.

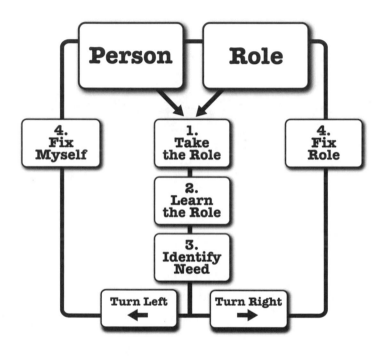

Step #4 is where the crucial difference lies between top performers and the rest. Less successful people mistakenly assume that they *can* develop natural thinking talents, so they focus on changing themselves by attempting to develop the natural talents the role requires. They mistakenly assume that with enough hard work and intelligence they can develop everything they need, so they set off trying to fix themselves. In other words, they *turn left* and focus on changing themselves while the job remains the same.

Geniuses, however, do the exact opposite. First, they appreciate the differences between talents and skills, so they don't spend their time trying to develop new natural talents. Second, they don't assume that the role is fixed either. Because of this, instead of focusing on changing themselves, they focus on changing the role.

In the diagram above, Geniuses *turn right* and focus on how to change the role so it doesn't depend on talents they don't already possess. They ensure their success depends on their talents, not their non-talents.

This is not to say that geniuses never turn left to focus on changing themselves. To develop new knowledge or skills, Geniuses absolutely turn left, but they understand that they are developing new skills—not new natural thinking talents.

If they need to acquire new knowledge or experience, Geniuses definitely do. But if the job calls for natural talents that they don't already possess, they either find another way to do that job, or they find another job. Geniuses may identify weaknesses between what they possess and what the role requires, but whereas non-geniuses seek to eliminate that weakness by developing themselves, Geniuses eliminate the weakness by removing their dependence on it.

~ *The single biggest differentiating characteristic of a Genius is the habit of turning right far more than turning left.* ~

The Myth of Strengths and Weaknesses

There is a myth about strengths and weaknesses that states that we all naturally possess them. In reality, we don't. No human possesses any single strength or weakness. What we *do* possess are natural talents and non-talents, but these are not the same as strengths and weaknesses.

Don't get me wrong, I'm not one of those who thinks it is too negative to tell someone he or she has a weakness and wants to call it "an opportunity for development." I actually dislike this phrase, because more often than not, it supports the incorrect view that someone can fix a weakness by developing a new natural talent for something. If one of my clients is suffering from a weakness, I tell him or her straight up. But the key is that this weakness isn't natural, it is *manufactured*.

Weaknesses and strengths don't exist naturally, only talents and non-talents. If, however, I rely on a non-talent, then I create a weakness for myself. Likewise, if I don't rely on my talents then they are never strengths for me. In this way, I manufacture strengths and weaknesses.

In other words, you are ultimately in control of your strengths and weaknesses. You may be born with talents and non-talents, but you are in charge of whether or not those talents and non-talents are used to become strengths or weaknesses. When you allow your success to depend on your talents, you create strengths. When you allow your success to depend on your non-talents, you create weaknesses.

This might seem like I'm talking about some minor, semantic difference, but I assure you that this is much more than a simple play on words. Understanding this concept requires a total change of perspective. Most people buy into the myth that they *possess* their strengths and weaknesses and fail to understand that they don't actually possess them, they create them. The power is theirs as to whether these strengths and weaknesses exist or not.

The thing that controls how these potentials turn out is how you apply yourself. Just as Mom used to say, "I brought you into this world, and I can take you out," so you, too, bring your weaknesses into this world, and you, too, can take them out. But instead of trying to take them out by developing new natural talents, you're simply going to remove your dependency on them.

Think of talents and non-talents like two boxes. The first box contains a gift and comes wrapped in pretty gift paper with a bow. The second box contains trouble and is marked *Pandora's Box*. Regardless of the contents, though, each box only contains potential. The first box is only potential for good, the latter only potential for bad. Nothing happens until you actually open the boxes. If you never open the gift box, you never receive the gift contained inside. Likewise, if you never open Pandora's Box, you never suffer the consequences. Talents and non-talents work in very much the same way.

This understanding is important, because once you realize that you create your strengths and weaknesses, you realize that you are in control. You realize that you don't have to suffer from weaknesses which were given to you and about which you can do nothing. You are in control because, while you definitely have non-talents, nothing in the universe states that you have to depend on them. And if you don't depend on them, then they aren't weaknesses, are they?

Geniuses understand this. They know that they are the only ones responsible for whether they benefit from strengths or suffer from weaknesses. They do not allow their success to become dependent on their non-talents.

Instead, they focus on *maximizing* their dependence on talents and *minimizing* their dependence on non-talents.

The elder statesman of management, Peter Drucker, said much the same thing when he told leaders, "Your job is to make the strengths of your people effective and their weaknesses irrelevant." He didn't talk about correcting their weaknesses by developing new natural talents. He championed making them irrelevant by not depending on non-talents.

The Unasked Question

A great example of someone manufacturing a weakness can be found in the story of Beth, an executive coach. On a recent teleconference with Beth and twelve other coaches, as we talked about the concept of manufacturing weaknesses, Beth spoke up with a challenge and said that sometimes you don't have a choice but to rely on a non-talent. She went on to explain that she couldn't turn right in one aspect of her job, and that it was "just a part of [her] job."

The part of her role she was referring to was the task of selling. As an independent business consultant, in order to grow her practice, she had to find new clients. Beth's natural talents, however, didn't support the typical definition of "selling." She didn't like prospecting, she wasn't comfortable cold calling or closing aggressively. Her natural talents were such that much of what it takes to *sell* was just not a strong suit for her.

Even though she knew selling wasn't her strength, she bought into the same belief that so many others do—that the role is the role; that there are just certain aspects of a job that are beyond reproach, and there is nothing you can do to turn right or change the role.

As a result, she had been turning left for years, trying to fix herself and create a natural ability for selling where none existed previously. She had taken sales training programs, read sales development books, and tried everything that other consultants had said worked for them. No matter how many times she turned left, though, she didn't see any real improvements.

By the time we were talking she had reconciled herself to the fact that sales was just a part of the role, and if she wanted to be an executive coach she was just going to have to sell—even if it meant manufacturing a weakness.

Think about it. Even though she knew she wasn't very good at selling, it never really dawned on her that she could turn right and eliminate that aspect of her role altogether. That's how engrained the belief is that the role is the role. That's how programmed we all are to think, "If something isn't right, it's me that has to change."

What Beth was missing was the fact that she didn't have to sell. Her simple yet significant error was that she bought into the message that the whole world had sold her. From books on how to start your own consulting practice to experts and lectures on being a successful entrepreneur, Beth had been told that in order to succeed as an independent executive coach she would *have* to also be a good sales person.

The only problem with that concept is that not one of those sources out there knew anything about Beth's natural talents. There was an entire world of experts and mentors ready to instruct Beth on how to succeed by following the path they had followed. All of them failed, however, to appreciate that perhaps Beth had to take her own path to reach the same objective.

When I asked Beth, "Why do you try to be a sales person?" she said, "So I can grow my coaching practice." Then I asked her, "If your objective is to be a great coach, then why are you trying to be a great sales person?" Beth's reply was, "Because that's what the job requires."

And there you have it. Beth had fallen into the same trap so many others had fallen into as well. Like many of us, Beth was conditioned to believe there was only one best way to fulfill her role, and with so many people telling her the same thing (e.g. you have to sell), she never imagined questioning it.

The simple solution for Beth was to stop trying to be a sales person and instead just focus on being what she wanted to be—a successful coach. She had not asked herself, "How do I achieve my objective of growing my practice in a manner that doesn't involve my having to perform heavy sales activity?" However, once she asked that question, once she focused on the overall objective instead of the conventional path to it, she started coming up with all kinds of answers. It wasn't that the answers were terribly difficult to come by, just that she hadn't thought to ask the question.

Once the right questions were being asked, though, the answers started to flow. It turns out that most successful coaches do very little sales-based marketing. Instead, they follow the education-based marketing approach. Sales-based methods may work fine when you are selling a commodity, but not so much for professional services. Ask yourself, have you ever gone to a physician whose office called your house to ask if you were sick?

Once Beth was focusing her effort in the right place (i.e. figuring out how to grow her business without selling), she found a whole host of resources to help her create an education-based marketing program that had her authoring articles, lecturing as an expert, and sharing a newsletter with a growing subscription base in which clients were coming to her.

Was it any less work? No, it wasn't, but if you ask Beth, she'll tell you that it felt like a whole lot less effort, because she was relying on what she loved to do and did well (speak, lecture, educate) and growing her practice at the same time.

In the end, Beth learned that by turning right and changing her role, instead of turning left in an attempt to change herself, she was much more successful, happy and satisfied with what she did. Her practice is up 250% now, compared to this time last year, by the way.

Geniuses don't have more talents than anyone else. They are just as flawed and imperfect as the next person. Geniuses don't have fewer non-talents, either. They just have fewer weaknesses, because they are very aware of their non-talents, and they do a damn good job of not depending on them.

The level of success these Geniuses achieve is hard to argue with, so there is much we can learn from their view on strengths and weaknesses. They achieve significantly more success with less effort, while finding more passion, satisfaction and happiness. And they do this by maximizing their dependence on natural talents and minimizing dependence on non-talents.

Genius Thoughts

Here are some thoughts from some of the Geniuses I interviewed for this book, particularly as they relate to the two acquired skills of self-awareness and authenticity.

Marshall Goldsmith on Self-Awareness

"I think I am very aware of my strengths. My strengths are being very good at coaching others—specifically the teaching aspect of coaching due to my love and passion for teaching. I love teaching and I'm very good at it because, in part, I am very good at taking complex concepts and organizing them in a simple way that is easy to understand. This is one of the gifts I have for teaching others. My job is helping others set realistic goals, evaluating them in those goals, and teaching them how to reach them better. As for my weaknesses, I am not good at managing people, so I just don't do it. I have lots of weaknesses, I just don't do them and I have no interest in correcting them. I constantly try to refine the strengths I have, but that doesn't mean I try to develop things I don't already possess. One of the keys to my success is that I've been able to find a role, or create one actually, that depends primarily on the natural talents I already possess."

Michael Lorelli on Authenticity

"I'm a perpetual optimist. I've always been called incredibly optimistic, and it shows in the energy that a great leader brings, and I can't imagine that it doesn't impact the bottom line significantly. In my 30s and 40s, there was a huge focus on learning and on what HR called our 'developmental needs,' and we spent a ton of time trying to become excellent in our non-talents. In the end, though, we all eventually just let most of that work fall by the wayside and migrated back to maximizing our strengths.

"I focus much more on my talents than my weaknesses. I know what my talents are for and I know what they are not for, and I'll hire a great COO to manage the details and pennies and micromanage that which should be micro-managed. Those are things that I choose not to spend my time on because I know I will never be great at them. I hire the right person to handle it, as opposed to trying to train myself to do those things better. It's simply not in my DNA, so I try to align myself better, not change myself. I believe in supplementing non-talents through others and delegation."

Short Thoughts: Mind-Fields

In the classes I teach, I like to use lots of physical analogies, because they help you connect a new concept to one you either already know or can more easily understand. When it comes to understanding the general concept for the two different approaches for dealing with weaknesses, I like to think of two different paths through a minefield.

Imagine you are a soldier tasked with getting from point A to point B. You look at your map and determine the best route to take to achieve your objective, and you start out on that path. Along the way, however, you come upon a minefield.

At this point you have two choices. You could choose option A, whereby you stick to your original path but stop to defuse each mine as you come to it. Or you could choose option B, whereby you simply walk around the minefield. Which would seem the most advantageous and expeditious? Most people would choose option B because it is faster and less risky.

Unfortunately, in real life most people are taught to choose option A. They are given an objective, determine a path to it and start down it. If along the way they realize that they have a weakness (a mine), instead of changing their path they stop to try and fix that weakness (defuse the mine). This is exactly what people do when they turn left and try to develop new natural talents.

The process of becoming a genius doesn't lie in becoming an expert at defusing mines or fixing weaknesses. It comes in being an expert in plotting a course that bypasses the mines altogether. If you choose Option A, you manufacture a liability or a hazard. When you choose Option B, the mines are still dangerous, but since your path to success doesn't take you through the minefield, they remain only potential hazards.

This book is about helping you discover potential mental obstacles so you can plot a course around them instead of through them. In the end, this course is much faster, easier and less likely to blow up in your face.

R Chapter 3 Review

Chapter 1:
- "The Problem" is an epidemic of people that feel unfulfilled, dissatisfied and frustrated with their performance.

Chapter 2:
- To find out why, we created the Genius Project, and what we found were two key things:
  - There is no one "Genius Talent"; and
  - Self-Awareness and Authenticity are present in higher levels in the best performers.

Chapter 3:
- The myth of strengths and weaknesses supports our turning left instead of right.
- Geniuses turn right significantly more than they turn left.

CG Chapter 3 Gut Check

Name three weaknesses that you have (with regard to performing—
not "chocolate"):

1. _____

2. _____

3. _____

Now consider these weaknesses, and ask yourself how you manage to
manufacture them by depending on a non-talent. What responsibilities do you have in your role that create reliance on these non-talents
and create these weaknesses?

1. _____

2. _____

3. _____

How could you change your role so these weaknesses went away,
becoming only potential weaknesses once again?

1. _____

2. _____

3. _____

What percentage of the time do you think you turn left to fix yourself
compared to turning right to fix the job?

I turn left ?% of the time:

 0%   10%   20%   30%   40%   50%   60%   70%   80%   90%   100%

Did you say that more than 50% of the time you try to fix yourself,
develop new natural talents, or allow the job to depend on something
that is not a natural talent for you?

How do you justify being inauthentic like this?

_____

_____

_____

_____

_____

_____

_____

_____

_____

_____

_____

_____

_____

_____

_____

CHAPTER 4

What Happens When You Turn Left or Right

In the course of doing the research for the Genius Project, one of the things we wanted to understand better was what the real implications of The Problem were. What were the effects of such a large percentage of people being dissatisfied with their results, frustrated with their constant attempts to improve and feeling unfulfilled with their jobs in general? The impact is sobering!

Just imagine what The Problem means to a single company. Think of the profits left on the table by a company with a workforce that is uninspired, unmotivated and unfulfilled. Imagine the impact on one company if even 10% of the workforce suffers from The Problem. What does it do to service levels when those who are serving don't feel well served themselves?

When you move past one company to all the companies out there, how many millions of dollars are wasted on remedies that fail to address the real problem, and how many billions of dollars are never realized in the first place because a significant percentage of the workforce's true potential is never realized?

As significant as that question is, the problem is most destructive at the personal level.

At the Human Level

Today, Gretchen Dougherty is one of the top sales people in her company, but this wasn't always the case. Her company sells home security systems, and Gretchen's job as an inside sales agent is to prospect over the phone to schedule home visits where a field sales representative gives a security consultation (otherwise known to you and me as a sales pitch). She spends her days sitting in a cubicle dialing out to homeowners trying to get them to schedule a home evaluation. Gretchen gets paid a sales commission for every security system that is sold as a result of appointments she schedules.

When she first took the job, she was taught that sales is a numbers game. Management told her that she had to make a specific number of outbound calls every day in order to beat the odds. The best sales people in the company made approximately ninety to 100 phone calls per day and ended up scheduling three to five field appointments, out of which one would normally sign a contract. Management really stressed to her the importance of making a high volume of calls. Each sales person even had a daily call quota.

The problem is that Gretchen had a very different talent set than most of the other sales people. Unlike the majority of them, she had a very high natural talent for empathy. It was this empathy that actually got in her way, because while other sales people would spend no more than a few minutes trying to push for an appointment, Gretchen found herself talking to people for five, ten, even fifteen minutes or more. She knew she had to generate a high volume of calls, so she was constantly turning left and trying to fix herself by suppressing her natural empathy and not connecting too much with the person on the other end of the phone.

When she did this, she was not being true to who she was. She was awkward and preoccupied with watching the all-holy clock that sat next to her computer. The more she tried to ignore her natural tendencies and think differently, so she could follow the script and stick to a time limit, the more awkward and ineffective she became.

Gretchen was in trouble. She wasn't performing well at all, and the top question on her management's mind was whether she would quit before they fired her. She was definitely ready to quit when I first met her.

After I spoke with Gretchen, it became clear right away that the issue seemed to be a poor fit between her natural talents and her role. Because of this, I gave her a battery of assessments to help understand what her true talents were and how well they were aligned with her existing role. One of these assessments was the Attribute Index that we used in the Genius Project.

The moment I saw the results, it was obvious to me what the problem was, and Gretchen confirmed. Her extremely high empathy was causing her to want to connect with people too much, at least too much to allow her to meet her daily call quota. The rest of the sales people in the company didn't have anywhere near Gretchen's level of empathy. Getting on and off the phone as quickly as possible wasn't a problem for them, but it was proving to be a big problem for Gretchen. She felt bad about talking *at* people instead of talking *with* them. The result was that Gretchen was trying to be something she wasn't, and it was negatively affecting her performance in a big way.

Luckily, her company was pretty open-minded about how to fix the problem. They had spent a lot of money training Gretchen, and given that they were already suffering from a high human turnover rate, they gave me the latitude I needed to attempt to correct the problem.

What did I do? I simply told Gretchen to turn right and figure out how to be true to who she was. Once she opened up to the possibility that she could change the way she worked instead of the way she naturally thought, she was able to make adjustments to how she went about achieving her goals.

I asked her how she would do the job if she were in charge. I said, "Just do you." As a result, Gretchen turned right and sought to change her role—not herself. She decided she would not put any time limit on the calls she made to prospects. She got rid of the clock on her desk and decided that she would not have a daily call quota, or any call quota for that matter—just a single quota for how many appointments she scheduled.

When she did this a very interesting thing happened. Gretchen, instead of suppressing her natural tendencies, started letting them guide her. She spent much more time with those she talked with. She got to know them and to understand their needs much better. She once even told me about a call where she learned about the caller's teenage daughter, what her name was, how often she was home alone, where she was going to college, and even what she was majoring in. This was typical of the level of communication Gretchen was having with the people she talked with. She was really connecting with these people.

Instead of trying to force herself to ignore her empathy, Gretchen was now using that natural talent to connect with people on a much deeper level than the rest of the sales reps were. Doing so meant that she spent a lot more time with each person, and made only as few as twenty to twenty-five calls per day. But doing so also meant that she was establishing relationships with people; relationships that were returning results. Despite the fact that Gretchen was making less than 20% of the calls the other reps were, she still averaged to book three to five appointments each day. Even better than that, instead of the company average of one signed contract for every five appointments, Gretchen was averaging two signed contracts for every five appointments.

Pretty soon, the field sales people were fighting to see who would get to call on the appointments that Gretchen had scheduled, because they knew their odds of making a sale were a lot better.

The lesson here is that by turning left and becoming inauthentic Gretchen was hurting her performance. When she started turning right, though, and became authentic, not only did her performance reach the expected levels, but actually exceeded them. When she was inauthentic, she was no more satisfied with her job than the job was satisfied with her. Now that she is authentic, she views her job as a vehicle for her passion for meeting and helping people, and now she is as satisfied with the job as it is with her.

If you ask the field sales representatives whom they want booking their appointments, they will tell you, "Gretchen, man, she is a genius at finding people who buy."

The Long X

Gretchen is a good example of someone living on the left side of what I call the Long X, which is a simple but effective way of understanding the relationship between authenticity and performance and how much effort you have to put in versus the results you get back.

When you are authentic, you are making sure that the work you do, and how you do it, is well aligned with your natural talents. The result is that you achieve more success with less effort. When you are inauthentic, you allow your success to be dependent on your non-talents, and what results you do get take inordinate amounts of effort.

The benefits of being authentic are significant, not only from the perspective of how well you perform, but also with regard to the satisfaction and sense of fulfillment you get. Basically, being authentic is much more productive. You just do better when you are authentic.

The diagram on the following page gives you an easy way to understand the differences between being authentic and being inauthentic and the effects this has on how much effort you feel you put in and how much performance you get out.

The discussion on effort is a qualitative one, not a quantitative one. It is more on effort as a feeling, not necessarily as an amount of work. To say that geniuses don't put in as much effort is not to say they don't work hard, just that when they align their talents with their work, it doesn't *feel* like effort. Think about it. We're talking about aligning your natural talents so that when you work from them, the results come naturally.

Frances Hesselbein, the founding director of the Peter F. Drucker Foundation and former CEO of Girls Scouts of America, talks about effort in the following way: "Success is about finding your passion and being true to it. People like me have never had a job. When you are doing things that align with your talents and strengths, you don't consider it work, it is your passion."

When you are authentic, the effort you feel yourself putting in, from a subjective point of view, is much less. Instead of "effort," you put in passion, you put in desire—you put in *you*. When you are

The Long X

The Long X is a term that describes the level of results you get when you are inauthentic as opposed to authentic. When you are inauthentic you are inverted and feel like the effort that you put in exceeds the results you get back. When you become authentic you become converted and you start to feel like you get back more results than the effort you felt you had to put in. Authenticity is the Geniuses' secret to consistently high 5th level performance.

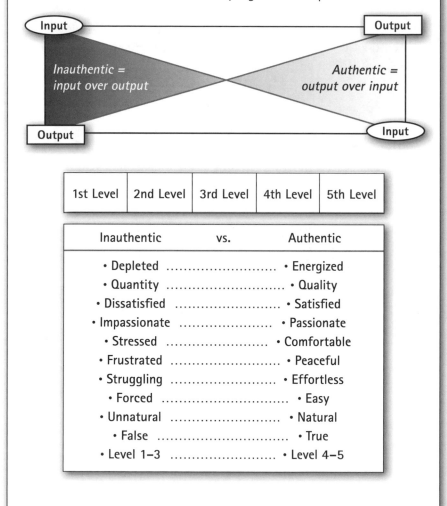

inauthentic, you are forcing yourself to be something you are not, and *that* feels like effort.

Best-selling business author Bill Brooks once wrote, "We may be able to force ourselves, with mature will and self-discipline, to do certain unpleasant things in order to get very desirable results. But it is almost impossible to force ourselves to do so consistently."

When you think about the Long X, just remember: sometimes less really is more. When you are inauthentic, you achieve less with more effort and stress, but when you are authentic, you achieve more with less effort and stress.

How do you feel in your role right now? Do you feel upside down? Are you on the wrong side of the Long X, always having to put in more effort than you get out in results? What score did you give yourself on the Problem Pre-Assessment under the Effort/Ease category?

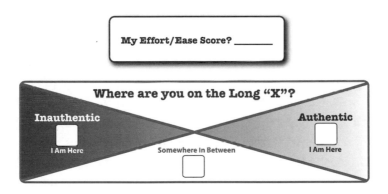

Beyond Performance

The effects of being inauthentic reach far beyond simple performance issues. The more disconcerting aspects of being inauthentic are what it does to you emotionally and even physically.

Being inauthentic is stressful, and I don't mean "healthy stress" (eustress), I mean "harmful stress" (distress). Being inauthentic in the first place is stressful enough—telling yourself you aren't good enough, trying to be something you are not, etc.—but the lack of performance that usually results from being inauthentic adds even more stress.

And when you look at what modern medicine is just now learning about the impact of stress on the human body (let alone psyche), the effects are startling.

According to Dr. Leon Pomeroy, the founding president of the International Academy of Preventive Medicine, "Psychological and emotional stress can gravely affect the human body in many negative ways. Stress triggers an overdose of hormones like epinephrine and cortisol that, over time, can become toxic to the human body. Chronic stress negatively affects your body's ability to regulate it's own processes (homeostasis). Your ability to absorb nutrients, lose weight and even fight off infections are negatively affected. Even the chemistry of sleep is disrupted by chronic stress, and sleep deprivation itself only aggravates the symptoms even more."

Some common side effects of chronic stress on the physical body are:

- The immune system: Under stress, the body becomes more vulnerable to illnesses, from colds and minor infections to major diseases. If you have a chronic illness, stress can make the symptoms even worse.
- Cardiovascular disease: Stress is linked to high blood pressure, abnormal heartbeat (arrhythmia), problems with blood clotting, and hardening of the arteries (atherosclerosis). It is also linked to coronary artery disease, heart attack, and heart failure.
- Muscle pain: People who are stressed often have neck, shoulder and lower back pain. This may be caused by constant tension in the muscles because of stress. Stress also affects rheumatoid arthritis.
- Stomach and intestinal problems: Recent research indicates that stress plays a significant role in gastro esophageal reflux disease (GERD), peptic ulcer disease, and irritable bowel syndrome.

In addition to the negative physiological impact it has on your body, chronic stress can adversely affect your thoughts and decisions.

Psychological signs and symptoms usually associated with stress can be:

- Increased irritability or sensitivity to minor disturbances.
- Feeling jumpy or exhausted all the time.
- Difficulty concentrating.
- Worrying about insignificant things.
- Frustration and a feeling of something being wrong somewhere, but not sure where.

Granted, being inauthentic is not the only cause of stress in our lives, but being inauthentic definitely adds to our level of stress. There are a lot of things that cause stress, and a lot of factors that determine our ability to handle it, but we do know that being inauthentic—having to work in an uncomfortable job, having to modify your behavior all day long, constantly having to apply a non-talent—is definitely stressful.

The more inauthentic you are, the more frustrated you get with your results, the less fulfilled you feel in your work, the less success you achieve, and the more stress you will suffer. And that's bad news for your physical and psychological health and wellbeing.

I once worked with one of our consultants to help a client of hers whose corporate world headquarters were in Manhattan. This company was suffering from The Problem on a systemic level. They had morale issues, health and wellness problems, increased sickness and absenteeism, and a whole host of performance issues caused in large part by the level of stress in their office. It was so significant that one day the executive vice president of Human Resources told us, "On average, an ambulance pulls up in front of our building 350 times a year."

Now I'm sure there are a fair number of accidental staples to be removed from fingers and twisted ankles on stairwells and other reasons for an ambulance to show up at an office with thousands of employees, but 350 times a year? Unfortunately too large a majority of these visits were for people with chest pain, who had passed out or were feeling so sick they felt they needed an ambulance. This was a workplace filled with way too much stress. Was all of this stress from people being inauthentic? Of course not. Was it a major contributing factor? You bet!

To say that people are physically damaging themselves, even dying, from stress is not hyperbole. The Problem is a major contributor to this concern.

The Neglected Child

Outside of the physiological effects of stress, turning left and being inauthentic takes something out of you emotionally. When you attempt to fill a role that requires you to have natural talents that you don't have, you are pretending to be something you are not. This pretending is basically like turning your back on your own self. In a way you disrespect yourself when you are inauthentic. Instead of adding to you, pretending to be something other than what you are actually subtracts from you. In the end, all that is left, when you look back, is time spent (perhaps a lifetime unfortunately) playing a role, pretending to be someone else.

But your inner self isn't stupid. What are you saying to your inner self when you pretend to be someone else? Deep down somewhere, pretending like this tells your inner self that your real self must not be good enough—that *you* aren't good enough. Pretending to be something else is like ignoring what you really are.

Let's imagine for a moment that your inner self were an outer self. Let's make it a whole other person actually, and that person is your own child who looks to you for love, recognition and validation. What would the effect on that child be if you neglected her? How would that make her feel? It would probably make her feel as if she wasn't worthy. By ignoring the child, you would make her feel not good enough.

Being inauthentic has the same subconscious effect on your inner self. By ignoring who you truly are, and pretending to be someone else, you are in effect telling yourself that you are not good enough. You are ignoring yourself in favor of what you need to be as defined by a job. And for what—some job, some role, some set of competencies that were written by an HR generalist somewhere?

There is a most remarkable quote from Maryanne Williamson that captures the fear many suffer when it comes to admitting their own true potentials. Nelson Mandela used it in his 1994 inaugural speech, and it goes:

> Our deepest fear is not that we are inadequate. Our deepest fear is that we are powerful beyond measure. It is our light, not our darkness that most frightens us. We ask ourselves, Who am I to be brilliant, gorgeous, talented, fabulous? Actually, who are you not to be? You are a child of God. Your playing small does not serve the world. There is nothing enlightened about shrinking so that other people won't feel insecure around you. We are all meant to shine, as children do. We were born to make manifest the glory of God that is within us. It's not just in some of us; it's in everyone. And as we let our own light shine, we unconsciously give other people permission to do the same. As we are liberated from our own fear, our presence automatically liberates others.

Respect for an individual can take no higher form than self-respect. Living an inauthentic life, failing to seek to know you or knowing yourself but then neglecting that self, is the greatest form of disrespect we can commit against ourselves.

~ The act of ignoring your own true self, in the name of reaching your own true potential, is the greatest act of folly. ~

God's Mistake or Yours

Here's another way to look at it. To assume that you—at your very core—need to *fix* yourself requires the presupposition that you must be broken, and that implies that God screwed up. Feel free to substitute whatever spiritual belief you have, but it won't likely change the concept. Think about it. If you believe that at your very core the way you were made is insufficient to achieve great success, then you have to admit that you view yourself as flawed.

Now I'm not talking here about developing new knowledge or skills (things that you aren't born with but must acquire). I'm talking about a belief that "I need fixing." Acquiring new knowledge and experience is great. That's a prerequisite for anyone's success, and something all 5th-level performers constantly do. But when you attempt to fix *who* you are instead of fixing *how* you are, then you must first think who you are is insufficient. And if you think that, then you can't avoid the questions, "Who screwed up? Who made me insufficient?"

In reality, it's not what you are at your very core that needs work, but how you apply yourself that needs fixing. You have a completely unique and incredibly powerful set of natural talents, so it's not what raw materials you have to work with that you should be concerned about. What you should be focused on is how you apply those raw materials.

~ If you need to fix anything, it is the way you apply you—not you! ~

Geniuses understand this. They don't view themselves as flawed, rather any flaws they see come in how they apply their talents. Because of this radically different perspective on themselves, when they focus on correcting flaws, those flaws are in their application of themselves, not in themselves. They don't try to change their talents, they change how those talents are applied.

In other words, God made you, but you decide what to do with yourself. If a problem exists in your life, it's not with the thing God created, but how you apply it.

I say all of this because there is a huge difference between thinking you are broken and realizing that you are just poorly aligned. The former is a racecar with a blown engine that must be completely rebuilt (broken). The latter is a perfectly good Ferrari trying to race in an off-road rally (poorly aligned).

~ Success in not about developing talent—it's about aligning it. ~

Illumination

The most vital aspect of awakening your authentic self is the recognition that you are inauthentic in the first place. To paraphrase one of Albert Einstein's famous quotes, "To continue to do the same thing yet expect different results is truly madness." Being inauthentic is actually a little "mad." One way of looking at inauthenticity is as a minor form of "madness," albeit one that all of us suffer from at one point or another.

Later in this book, we will help you identify exactly how you are being inauthentic, but your first big step—right here and right now—is to ask yourself, "How authentic am I?" The Danish philosopher, Soren Kierkegaard, said, "Face the facts of what you are, for that is what changes what you are." You have to face the fact that you are being inauthentic before you can stop being so. In many ways, I like to think that *illumination is 80% of remediation*. Oftentimes simply identifying and understanding the problem is the greatest step you take in resolving it.

Author Eckhart Tolle describes in his book, *A New Earth*, what Hinduism calls "Maya," or the veil of delusion. While I'm not talking about morality in this book, he makes a compelling argument for how to end an illusion by identifying it first. Tolle says, "You do not become good by trying to be good, but by finding the goodness that is already within you and allowing that goodness to emerge. But, it can only emerge if something fundamental changes in your state of consciousness. To replace one's own insanity is, of course, the rising of sanity, the beginning of healing and transcendence. The good news is that if you can recognize illusion as illusion, it dissolves. The recognition of illusion is also its ending. Its survival depends on your mistaking it for reality. In the seeing of who you are not, the reality of who you are [starts to] emerge."

In our discussion, let's substitute "Genius" for Tolle's "good." You do not become a genius by trying to be a genius, but by finding the genius that already exists within you and allowing it to emerge. To become authentic requires that you leave your state of inauthenticity. In other words, to replace one's own inauthenticity is the rising of authenticity.

Being authentic is about seeing what life can do through you, not to you. You do this by *releasing* you inner genius, not *creating* it. With self-awareness comes the tapping into an intelligence far greater than any book learning or experience can deliver. It is an ancient intelligence, refined through hundreds of thousands of years (in our genes, in our society, in our memes) and ideally suited to make you a genius in something.

You possess unique natural talents that are the result of everything learned by everyone who has come before you. Each of them has left some indelible reference to what they discovered. The trick is finding out what that something is and being honest enough with yourself to let go of your preconceived notions about how the rest of the world thinks you should be and follow your own path to who you are.

"To be yourself in a world that is constantly trying to make you something else is the greatest accomplishment."
~ RALPH WALDO EMERSON

Passion and Purpose

In one way, learning your talents and being authentic is the same as learning what your passions are and being true to them. When you are being true to your genius, you are being true to your passions. When you are doing what you love to do, and naturally do well, you are drawn to it.

Passion is the force that drives all successful people and actions, and being authentic is being passionate. In *The Eighth Habit*, author Stephen Covey talks about the importance that authenticity plays in passion. "The key to creating passion in your life is to find your unique talents and your special role and purpose in the world," says Covey.

Geniuses are passionate about their roles. Their roles are well aligned with who they are. They don't consider it work. They love what they do, and they would still do it even if they didn't have to. When you are engaged in work that taps into your talents and is fueled by your passion, therein lies your calling, your Genius. Covey goes on to say that, "There is a deep, innate, almost inexpressible yearning within each one of us to find our voice in life." I believe that voice he is talking about is your genius.

In the Flow

When you do all of this. When you openly and honestly acknowledge that God didn't screw up, and the only *mistake* has been in how you have applied what was given to you, when you stop neglecting your inner self, and once you have become truly authentic and begin to maximize the talents you already possess, you will find there is an almost mystical aspect to the performance you will achieve.

Basil King said, "Be bold, and mighty forces will come to your aid." I like to think that by being "bold" he meant daring to be who you are, and those "mighty forces" he talks about are your natural talents coming to your aid now that you have acknowledged them. They were always there, just hidden as untapped potential.

When you become authentic, though, and let those talents out, it is as if you are suddenly plugged into some invisible energy that powers your performance, and the results you get often elicit a feeling of "How did I do that? It didn't seem that hard."

When this happens—when you operate on the far right side of the Long X—you are in what I call *the flow*. Abraham Maslow talks about B-Cognition, or Peak Experiences, and these are times where people are in the flow. He describes people in peak experiences as being one with what they do. The two are not separate. The person is not "thinking" about doing it, they are just doing it. Athletes and artist commonly get in the flow, and the professional athletes I've worked with tell me that if they have to think about it, it's too late. In *First Break All The Rules*, author Marcus Buckingham describes this moment by saying, "Your whole brain seems to light up as if a whole bank of switches were suddenly flicked on."

Garry Titterton is a world-class ad guy and the author of the book, *Brand Storming*. He is also one of the geniuses I interviewed for this book. He has had phenomenal success in his profession, from leading the team that created a marketing promotion for Coca-Cola that generated a Guinness World Record-winning forty million entries to helping create the wildly successful and award-winning catch phrase, "I Can't Believe It's Not Butter."

In one of my discussions with Garry, he shared his thoughts on how self-awareness and authenticity have been a driving force

behind his success all of his life and what it means to him when he
is in the flow:

> I've always been very aware I think, at least compared
> to others I've known, of what my natural talents were for.
> I'm a very strategic person, and while I can be the detail-
> oriented guy who moves quickly and in a more tactical
> manner, I prefer to take the strategic approach and think
> big picture. I outsource the implementation of those strate-
> gies to others since that is not a strength for me. If I don't
> do this, if I make my success dependent on my ability to
> be the tactician, I am doing myself a disservice. When I
> am ignoring the strategic vision to implement actions, I
> feel I'm being untrue, and I am not in the flow. And when
> I'm not in the flow, I don't feel that sense of oneness with
> what I am doing. The results show too. When I'm not in
> the flow, results are just much harder to come by. I have an
> incredibly strong sense of this inner voice, and I've learned
> to trust and follow it, and it leads me to being in the flow
> more often than not. When I'm in the flow, my success
> comes so much more completely with so much less effort.
>
> As a young sportsman it was this sort of Zen thing where
> when I was in the flow (when the game was playing me), I
> did great and loved it, but when I wasn't in the flow (when I
> was trying to play the game) I did very poorly and didn't enjoy
> it at all. When you are being authentic and true to who you
> are, there is a harmony and rhythm not unlike music. You
> feel complete. There is a line in a Robert Browning poem[5]
> that says, 'On earth the broken arcs; in heaven the perfect
> round.' When I'm not being true to myself I feel like the
> broken arc, but when I'm being authentic and true, or when
> I'm in the flow, I feel like a complete circle—perfect (heaven).

When Garry talks about the Browning quote, he is describing what
I hear so often from others I work with. When they try to override their

---

[5] Browning's, *The Abt Vogler.*

natural talents, they feel broken, not whole and unfulfilled. They suffer from The Problem. When they let nature take its course, however, and they allow who they are to come to the surface, they feel complete, whole and fulfilled. They become Browning's "perfect round."

The real key to being very successful is to find ways to be in the flow more often than not. To give you a simple way to remember this lesson yourself, I give you a figure from my childhood that is the quintessential *authentic* character. As Popeye so famously said, "I yam what I yam and that's all that I yam." The Geniuses in our world wouldn't argue with him one bit, spinach or not.

Genius Thoughts

Here are some thoughts on Passion and Purpose from one of the Geniuses I interviewed for this book.

Frances Hesselbein on Authentic Passion

"Peter Drucker would say all the time, 'Your job is to make the strengths of your people effective and their weaknesses irrelevant!' I think I've always been very aware of my strengths and weaknesses. When I am at my best, it is when I am focusing on what I do best; when I am less effective, it is when I am ignoring those talents but choose to carry out those practices which rely on my non-talents. The thing to keep in mind is that success is a matter of how to be, not how to do. People like you and I have never had a job. They have been called to do what they do best. Warren Bennis calls it the leader within or the spirit within.

"When you are doing things that align with your talents and strengths, you don't consider it work. It is your passion. I think the purpose of a good leader is to mobilize people around a passionate mission, but it has to be in *their* way to reach their passion. Great leadership requires the best, and to be the absolute best you can't be false, you can't be trying to be great at something you aren't naturally great at."

| R | **Chapter 4 Review** |

Chapter 1:
- "The Problem" is an epidemic of people that feel unfulfilled, dissatisfied and frustrated with their performance.

Chapter 2:
- To find out why, we created the Genius Project, and what we found were two key things:
    - There is no one "Genius Talent"; and
    - Self-Awareness and Authenticity are present in higher levels in the best performers.

Chapter 3:
- The myth of strengths and weaknesses supports our turning left instead of right.
- Geniuses turn right significantly more than they turn left.

Chapter 4:
- The effects of the problem go beyond performance issues to include negative physical and emotional effects.
- Inauthenticity causes you to feel upside down, always putting in more effort than you feel you get back in results, and blocks you from your passions and being in the flow.

CG Chapter 4 Gut Check

How stressed would you say you are right now in life? (circle one)

Very Unstressed   1   2   3   4   5   *Very Stressed*

What's an example of a time when you were "in the flow"? What were you doing when this happened?

_____

_____

_____

What percentage of your week do you feel like you are in the flow? (circle one)

0%   10%   20%   30%   40%   50%   60%   70%   80%   90%   100%

When you are in the flow, is it through professional or personal activities? (circle one)

Professional   Personal   Both

This gut check is designed to help you think about your own levels of stress and your ability to get into the flow. Geniuses feel less stressed and find themselves in the flow more often than not.

CHAPTER 5

Why We Choose the Direction We Do

Why do so many people turn left instead of right? Why do people believe that the role is fixed and it is themselves that must change or be fixed to achieve better performance? Why are so many people around the world being inauthentic and suffering from The Problem?

This lack of authenticity stems from a flawed belief system concerning the value of the individual in today's organizations. The flaw I'm referring to is the lack of appreciation for the uniqueness and individuality of people. It is a flawed belief that finds the job as sacrosanct and the individual as sacrificial. It is a belief that the job's duties and responsibilities should remain fixed and that the individual is the one who should change to better fit the job.

Such beliefs are the primary cause of an individual becoming inauthentic, and they lie at the very heart of the struggles we've been discussing. To understand this flawed belief system we need to consider its origin—the industrial age.

Food, Stuff and Ideas

In 1758, a young Scotsman named James Watt was suffering from his own struggles. Having been mostly home schooled and not meeting the requirements of completing a formal apprenticeship, the local Glasgow Guild would not allow him to take up work in his chosen career as an instrument maker. Later that year, however, Watt was offered the opportunity to set up a small workshop at the University of Glasgow Scotland. Within four years, this unofficial instrument maker would create one of the most significant technological break-throughs of his time—a breakthrough that would fuel an entire world of change—one we're actually still feeling today.

What Watt invented was a new steam engine, and his work initiated a series of improvements in generating and applying power that transformed the world of work and would go on to power the industrial revolution.

With the advent of modern technology and machinery, very much driven by Watt's improved steam engine, the world shifted to an economy based on industrial manufacturing rather than farm-ing. The onset of the industrial revolution marked a major turning point in human society where nearly every aspect of daily life was eventually affected in some way, including how individual workers were valued.

The primary assets of the industrial economy were natural resources and the processes that transformed them into products and goods. People were not the primary asset in the industrial economy. In the early 1900s, if a worker quit the production line at Ford Motor Company, Henry Ford could replace him with another worker without so much as a hiccup in production.

That's because in the Industrial economy, a very small minority of the workforce was considered a knowledge worker. The vast major-ity were simply laborers, and companies relied on their ability to *do* more than to *think*. They were valued more for their bodies than for their minds.

This is important to us today because believe it or not, it was in this industrial era where the majority of the management principles we know today were actually created, including many of the core principles of how to value and manage people. The only problem with this, however, is that the industrial-era view on individual workers was less than ideal.

The conventional wisdom of the industrial economy was that all workers should do things the prescribed way, the way the company says. To achieve this, if the job required a worker to be able to do something, and the worker wasn't good at it, it was the worker who was expected to change to fit the role better, not the other way around.

Such beliefs were due in large part to the work of one Frederick W. Taylor, who is commonly known as the Father of Scientific Management. For those not familiar with Scientific Management, or Taylor himself, Frederick W. Taylor was one of the most influential thought leaders of the industrial era. His seminal work, *Scientific Management,* ushered in an entirely new paradigm on the "one best way" to manage people for optimal efficiency in an industrial era.

According to Dr. Stephen Byrum, author of *The Recovery and Sustainability of the Human Element in Modern Organizations,* "This short but incredibly powerful 80-page book would have as much impact on the world of business as Karl Marx's *The Communist Manifesto* or Mao's *Little Red Book* had on governments of the time."

With the addition of his other great work, *The Principles of Scientific Management,* Taylor would become a world-famous thought leader on how to manage people more effectively. Most of the great organiza tions of the industrial era became his followers. Whole governments even adopted his lessons.

The only problem with this, though, is that Taylor's work had a powerfully negative impact on people in general. Taylor saw the individual as a flawed element to be controlled. As absurd as it seems today, people were his greatest obstacle to higher organizational performance. While some scholars argue that it was not Taylor's intention, his work would have a terribly dehumanizing effect on the world's work forces. His writings, in too many instances, became the impetus for the eventual reduction of the worker to nothing more than the automatons of Orwell's *1984.*

Let me share some examples of Taylor's work with you so that you can get a better picture of how the industrial era saw the individual worker through Taylor's eyes:

- On instructing managers how to manage workers for optimal performance, Taylor stated, "You do it my way, by my standards, at the speed I mandate, and in so doing achieve a level of output I ordain, and I'll pay you handsomely for it, beyond anything you might have imagined. All you have to do is take orders and give up your way of doing the job for mine."
- In his famous tract *Shop Management*, Taylor wrote, "Each man must give up his own particular way of doing things, adapt his methods to the many new standards, and grow accustomed to receiving and obeying instructions covering details large and small, which in the past had been left to individual judgment. The workmen are to do as they are told."
- In Taylor's opinion, the workmen "didn't need to think at all."

You can start to see how any management principles developed in the industrial era, under Taylor's influence, turned out to be quite devoid of any appreciation for the individuality and uniqueness of any one person.

Like the agrarian era before it though, the industrial era eventually gave way to yet another new era—the intellectual era. With advances in modern technology, production capabilities, the globalization of competition and ever-tightening labor pools, the world has shifted to an economy that relies much more heavily on a person's mental ability than on their physical ability. In the intellectual age, people are the new raw material (their creativity, their knowledge, their talents). The real value of an employee in today's organizations is based on their ability to *think*, not *do*, and they are more valued for their minds than for their bodies.

Peter Drucker described the world as moving from "an economy of goods to an economy of knowledge." Drucker called this new economy the "age of the knowledge worker," wherein the most vital assets were not the raw materials and processes that transformed them, but the minds and intellects of individuals who created and controlled them.

Best-selling author Seth Godin does a great job of summarizing this shift by explaining, "We used to make food, and then we made things, now we make ideas."

Of course, while Taylor's approach may arguably have worked in his time, it doesn't translate very well to today's environment, where most of what an individual does is mental in nature. Having "one best way" for everyone to act universally may work well when you are putting widgets together, but not so well for a workforce of knowledge workers. Expecting everyone to conform to a standard way of "doing" is one thing. Having them conform to a standard way of "thinking" is quite another.

While the world has shifted from an industrial age to an intellectual one, many of the beliefs about how to value people have not shifted. The majority of today's management beliefs are very much the remnants of past industrial mindsets. In many ways, we're still practicing old management practices that just don't work anymore.

As author Stephen Covey says in *The Eighth Habit*, "We live in a Knowledge Worker Age but operate our organizations in a controlling Industrial Age model that absolutely suppresses the release of human potential."

This has created a legacy of dependence where people look to the company to tell them how to proceed, how to work and *how to be*. People have become dependant on those with management authority to decide how they should best do the job. They consent to being controlled, but unfortunately, all these remnants of the old industrial age do is prevent people from tapping into their own natural talents and Genius.

"In the space age the most important space is between the ears."
~ THOMAS BARLOW

A Legacy of Dependence

The effect of this failure to shift management principles has resulted in people still being viewed primarily as commodities, expenses or *labor*. Individuals themselves continue to adhere to an old paradigm of how to value themselves. They continue to believe that it is management who knows best how they should actually do the job. People continue to look to management to tell them the best way to work and how to be successful.

Basically, our heritage from the industrial era is a mind-set wherein it is up to management to determine the best way to do things, even the best talents to possess. The individual just needs to shut up and follow directions.

I know what you are thinking: "Yeah, but that was over a hundred years ago. Business today is nothing like that." Before you start to dismiss all of this as ancient history, you need to appreciate how this mentality of Command and Control survives even today in the basic DNA of most organizations.

Below are three examples of an industrial-era management principle—one that devalues the individual—that survives today:

1. Most companies have a Chief Executive Officer, a Chief Financial Officer, and even a Chief Operations Officer—but how many have a Chief People Officer. In other words, finances, operations and governance are still more important and require Chief positions to head these segments of business. People are usually the primary responsibility of a Vice President of Human Resources who reports to one of the other Chief officers.

2. Ask most companies where they record capital equipment purchases and payroll on their books, and the answer is almost always that capital equipment is listed as an investment and payroll almost always goes in the expense column. While the company may want to believe that people are their most important asset, they continue to practice an old belief as to how they manage that asset, at least from a financial perspective. Not much has changed from Taylor's view that

people are an expense and something to be reduced as much as possible.

3. If the company manufactures anything, I ask them, "What is the defect rate for the products you make compared to your human turnover rate?" All too often the defect rate is much lower than the human turnover rate. This just means that they do a far better job of production management than they do people management (i.e. they fail less with things than they do with people).

This is not at all to say that companies today are intentionally disvaluing their people. For the most part, they truly do appreciate that they are in an intellectual economy, and they really do believe that people are the most vital asset. But the very field of management itself is so founded in the industrial mentality in which it was born that it is hard to realize the flaws because we are standing on them. The foundation of today's management principles carries over much baggage from the industrial age.

We have inherited a significant legacy from Taylor that continues to drive management beliefs that undervalue the individuality of the person *and*, worse yet, cause the individual to undervalue themselves as well.

Sometimes, when you live inside of something, it's easy to take it for granted. A friend of mine, Dr. Rem Edwards, recently said that explaining such familiar things is like "trying to explain water to a fish." It's easy to miss this kind of "big-picture" insight, because we all exist within the very thing in question, the thing that is flawed. It's so big that we can completely forget we are inside of it.

The earth is a good example of how easy it is to take for granted something that is so basic, so large, that you become oblivious to it. You could easily go your entire life without realizing that you are spinning 1,000 miles per hour in a small circle and at 67,000 miles per hour around a much larger circle, but that's how fast the earth rotates and moves around the sun. It's easy to miss this fact because everything you see is moving along with you. There is no context that exists outside of your reality, so to you nothing is moving.

Today's management beliefs are much like this. They exist as such a basic part of our business lives that they are simply taken for granted. It's hard to see past them, or think outside of them.

Unfortunately, these beliefs continue to perpetuate workplaces where individuals depend on the organization to tell them not only what to do but how to do it—what the one best way should be.

The result of this legacy of management principles is a belief system that remains not because it makes sense, but simply because it's a basic part of the fabric of management practice. I call such beliefs *legacy beliefs.*

Legacy beliefs may or may not be valid anymore, but they are always beliefs from a time that is no more. The danger with them is that they exist simply because they have always existed. They are not in place on their own merit, but rather by default.

In many ways we have not really moved all that far from Taylor's dehumanizing view of the worker, because we as individuals continue to allow others to tell us how to be. Instead of being authentic, we allow ourselves to be put into roles with predetermined duties or responsibilities that completely fail to factor in our unique and individual talents and abilities. We allow others to force us into their "one best way" instead of divining our own (i.e. "my best way").

Chairman (Ret.) Joint Chiefs of Staff, General Colin Powell shared his thoughts on this problem in the December 1996 issue of *Management Review,* where he said, "In a brain-based economy, your best assets are people. We've heard this expression so often that it's become trite. But how many leaders really 'walk the talk' with this stuff? Too often, people are assumed to be empty chess pieces to be moved around by grand viziers. How many [leaders] immerse themselves in the goal of creating an environment where the best, the brightest, the most creative are attracted, retained and, most importantly, unleashed?"

Follow That Crowd

Another major reason why this legacy of dependence persists today is due to a basic human need to conform and fit in. Not only did past management beliefs engrain into us a belief that conforming was good, but our very nature as social creatures provided fertile ground for such a belief to take root and grow.

At our core, all humans have a basic fundamental need to belong. Evolution has taught us that survival and prosperity is more likely if we live and work together. When we agree on things and share common beliefs, values and attitudes, it is that much easier to live and work together. While some are obviously less conformist than others, for all of us there is some part of our upbringing that instills in us an urging to conform to the rules or expectations of other people. The more we see others behaving in a certain way or making particular decisions, the more we feel obliged to follow suit.

For example, most people will be much less willing to express their opinion if they believe they are in the minority. They will also be more vocal if they believe they are a part of the majority. Right or wrong, this is a basic part of being the social creatures we are.

According to Dr. Heather Williamson, a professor of social psychology at Virginia Commonwealth University, all humans have a basic need to want to fit in. One reason is called the Similarity Principle, which states, "We trust people who are like us or who are similar to people we like." She says, "When we are trying to decide whether to trust someone, we often do not have time to find out how trustworthy they actually are, so we take a short-cut by assuming that someone who is either similar to us or who is similar to someone we would trust can be trusted themselves."

"We seek similarity in beliefs, values, attitudes, ways of thinking, understanding and making decisions. Since we long to be trusted, it is in our best interest to be similar to others, and therefore we strive to conform, to fit in, to be like the rest," says Dr. Williamson.

Another reason we conform, according to Dr. Williamson, is due to a psychological phenomenon called Majority Influence. The degree of influence that this effect can have on us is surprisingly strong.

The Asch conformity experiments, performed by Dr. Solomon Asch in the 1950s, were a series of studies that starkly demonstrated the true power of conformity in social groups.

Dr. Asch asked groups of students to participate in a "vision test," but in reality, all but one of the participants were working with Asch, and the study was really about how the one remaining student would conform to the other students' behavior. All of the subjects were seated in a classroom and were presented with two cards (much like those below). One had on it a "standard" line; on the other were three comparison lines. They were asked to judge which of the comparison lines (A, B or C) were equal in length to the standard line.

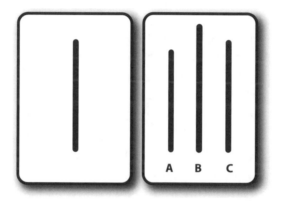

The group was told to announce their answers out loud, and the only *true* study participant would always be the last to answer. While this sole study participant didn't know it, the other students were secretly instructed to give the wrong answer. The idea was to see if the single study participant would conform to the group and give the same answer as the others, even when it was obviously the wrong answer.

When asked, all of those student's working with Professor Asch would state that the standard line was the same length as line A or B on the second card. Even though this was obviously wrong, the one student who wasn't a part of the Asch's control group would give this same incorrect answer a significant percentage of the time.

The results showed that 75% of the time, when the control group gave the wrong answer, the single participant knowingly gave a wrong answer as well. Clearly, participants did not want to stand out like a sore thumb or rock the boat, risking group disapproval. The lie they were telling was blatant, but they told it anyway so as not to stand out and risk being rejected or lose trust.

Due to majority influence, people are more likely to depend on others for the answer, and the more knowledgeable a person is, or the more authority they have, the more valuable they are as a resource. Thus, people are even more likely to follow managers or leaders.

Studies like these show us that one of our most basic human instincts is to follow the crowd, but that doesn't mean doing so is always the correct thing to do. Conformity can have either good or bad effects on people. Driving safely is an example of where conformity serves us well. Trying drugs because of peer pressure, however, is an example of where a need to fit in doesn't serve us well at all. The Asch experiments proved that people frequently followed the majority judgment, even when the majority was wrong.

Even though more and more people feel inauthentic in their roles today, and even though somewhere deep down inside it feels wrong somehow, they continue to do it anyway. When I say "wrong," by the way, I don't mean immoral. I mean that the way they are attempting to change who they are to fix weaknesses doesn't feel "right" to them, but their desire to fit in and not rock the boat plays a significant role in their deciding to follow the crowd anyway.

All of this only serves to reinforce the legacy of dependence we have on management telling us how to be successful, and is one of the main reasons so many people try to fix themselves instead of fixing their role. Becoming authentic and achieving the 5th level of performance requires that you stop following and start leading—yourself.

Short Thoughts: Taylor's Upside

In this chapter I've given Frederick W. Taylor a pretty hard time. This is not to say that he doesn't deserve it, and while his work is responsible for a tremendous amount of dehumanizing in the world, there were actually very positive things about his work as well. To be fair, I think we should at least shed a little light on those aspects.

Professor William Judge, the E.V. Williams Chair of Strategic Leadership & Professor of Strategic Management at Old Dominion

University, weighed in for this book on Taylor's positive effects in our world. According to Dr. Judge, Taylor made many contributions to our world, but the four most significant were:

- Efficiency: Coming out of an agrarian economy, there were no systems in place to streamline production on a grand scale and Frederick W. Taylor's work provided incredible efficiencies in manufacturing and industrial processes in general. Our modern world has reaped great benefits from his work in these areas.
- Mutual Benefits: Hidden among Taylor's writings is a good deal of content arguing strongly for the benefits of creating mutually beneficial environments where both the company and the worker benefited together—equally. The primary benefit he was concerned with was monetary, but at the turn of the century money was arguably the single greatest concern for most workers. Unfortunately, this is one of Taylor's messages that was ignored by many companies, when management decided to keep the profits for themselves.
- Worker Safety: At the time Taylor was becoming popular, working conditions in many organizations were horribly unsafe. Workers were exposed to incredibly high risk levels compared to today's standards. Taylor was very vocal about his belief that a healthy and safe worker is more productive. His arguments resulted in drastic improvements in worker safety, thus preventing unknown numbers of injuries and deaths. Even though his motivation for improving working conditions was driven strictly by a desire to improve productivity—and had nothing to do with benefiting humans—his work definitely improved working conditions around the world.
- Management Abuse: Taylor was a stickler for written protocols. As part of his Scientific Management Principles, he urged all companies to create rigid process guidelines that were to be written and formally established. Again, while his motives for doing this were to benefit productivity, the positive side-effect of written guidelines was that it helped constrain management abuse.

Frederick W. Taylor did indeed create a really big idea that shaped the world (and continues to do so), and we owe him much. Even though his ideas were misapplied and ended up contributing more to the problem than the solution in many ways, his processes for managing *things* remain some of the most influential work in the entire field of business management. Standard fixtures in organizations today, like TQM, Six-Sigma and the Toyota Way, would not exist were it not for the scientific standards that Taylor brought to the fledgling management theory of his time.

| R | **Chapter 5 Review**

Chapter 1:
- "The Problem" is an epidemic of people that feel unfulfilled, dissatisfied and frustrated with their performance.

Chapter 2:
- To find out why, we created the Genius Project, and what we found were two key things:
    - There is no one "Genius Talent"; and
    - Self-Awareness and Authenticity are present in higher levels in the best performers.

Chapter 3:
- The myth of strengths and weaknesses supports our turning left instead of right.
- Geniuses turn right significantly more than they turn left.

Chapter 4:
- The effects of the problem go beyond performance issues to include negative physical and emotional effects.
- Inauthenticity causes you to feel upside down, always putting in more effort than you feel you get back in results, and blocks you from your passions and being in the flow.

Chapter 5:
- Today's organizations have shifted from an industrial to an intellectual economy.
- Legacy beliefs left over from the old industrial economy cause dependence and inauthenticity that damages individual performance.

CG   Chapter 5 Gut Check

Think of a time in your life where you depended on the company to tell you how to be successful. What is one talent that you don't think you possessed naturally but that you were told you needed in order to succeed?

What was that talent?_____

What did you do to try and acquire that natural talent? _____

_____

How much effort did you put into acquiring this natural talent? (circle one)

Very Little   1   2   3   4   5   A Ton

How did that work for you in the end? (circle one)

I Improved Little to None   1   2   3   4   5   I Became a Genius.

CHAPTER 6

How to Choose the Right Direction

There is a famous passage in Plato's dialogue, *The Republic*, where Glaucon says to Socrates, "Now, old man, you have talked about the problem aplenty—now tell us the solution." I think I've talked about the problem aplenty as well, so now let's dedicate ourselves to just one thing...the solution.

Before you can turn right and change your role to align with your abilities better, you must first know what your natural talents are, and are not. Over the years that I have been helping people improve their performances through a better understanding of how they think and make decisions, I've worked personally with over 10,000 individuals. While not all of these people were being inauthentic, of course, a great many were, so I had to create a system to help them develop a better level of self-awareness, put an end to their own legacy of dependence, and learn how to become more authentic.

In addition to helping individuals do this, I've also taught over 1,400 professional counselors, consultants, managers, psychologists and educators this same process. So not only do I personally know how the process works, but many others have proven it works as well.

The result is an effective and easy-to-understand system that will help you break any legacy of dependence, re-discover your natural talents and finally become authentic to them so that you can reach the 5th level of performance.

While the system has been around for some time, in honor of this new book, I've given it a brand new name. I now call it the "5th-Level Performance Program," and by following it you will take control over your direction in life and your own success. This program will teach you that you are in control, and you can take yourself anywhere you want if you understand who you are and how you should best get there.

> *"You have brains in your head. You have feet in your shoes.*
> *You can steer yourself any direction you choose."*
>
> ~ Dr. Seuss

The 5th-Level Performance Program

Unlike many training and development programs, the 5th-Level Performance Program does not start with the false assumption that you need to change *who* you are, because you are not flawed in the first place. The only thing this program seeks to change is *how* you are, because the only flaw in your life to this point has been how you apply yourself.

The 5th-Level Performance Program consists of four main sections, or what I call Revolutions. The revolutions in the 5th-Level Performance Program are:

- Pre-Revolution—creating the right conditions for your next revolutions;
- Revolution #1—Know Thyself (Socrates)—becoming more fully self-aware;
- Revolution #2—Choose Thyself (Kierkegaard)—breaking with convention to find your authentic path; and
- Revolution #3—Create Thyself (Mirandola)—turning right and actually becoming authentic.

The 5th-Level Performance Program you are about to begin is designed to help you assess your level of satisfaction and success, align what you do naturally well with what you do for a living and overall improve your satisfaction, passion and success in life. Basically, it's designed to help you eliminate The Problem in your life. Together we'll either improve your existing roles, or we'll help you create better ones. At its core, this program is designed to help you either love what you do or go do what you love.

Pre-Revolution

"If you don't change your beliefs, your life will be like this forever. Is that a good thing?"

~ DR. ROBERT ANTHONY

In order for anything to evolve the conditions must be right. All the potential in the world might be lying in wait inside you, but if the conditions aren't right then all of that potential will never be realized. You have hidden within you infinite potential, but the principle condition that must be present in order for you to realize this potential is a belief system that supports your success—not a legacy of dependence. You have the freedom to control your own destiny, but you must believe this before you can actually take control.

Who's In Charge

Most likely, if The Problem is a significant one for you, your current belief system allows you to suffer from your own legacy of dependence. If you depend on the company, or the world, to tell you how to succeed, then before you start becoming more self-aware you need to examine your own belief system about who's in charge of your own success. The question you must ask yourself is, "Who is in charge of me?"

The first common problem with many inauthentic people is that they have a belief that the company or the outside world has more control than they do over their lives. There is a term in psychology called "Locus of Control," and it speaks to a belief about whether the outcomes of our actions are contingent on what we do or on events outside of our personal control.

Authentic people tend to have a much greater belief that they have control over their life and destiny. They have an internal locus of control. More inauthentic people, however, tend to have an external locus of control so they share a common belief that they are less in control of what happens to them.

The way individuals interpret such events has a profound affect on their psychological well-being. If people feel they have no control over future outcomes, they are less likely to seek solutions to their problems. It isn't the problems that I'm saying we have control over, mind you. Of course we can't control natural disasters, or birth defects, or being laid-off. But how we respond to such events—the solutions we create to the situations and adversities life throws at us—these are things we do control. Having an internal locus of control means believing that you can make a difference in how your life turns out. It means believing in your heart that you have a lot of influence over how successful you are, no matter the obstacles.

This is why it is crucial that you start to believe in your own ability to control your life, your performance and your success. You must stop depending primarily on the "one best way" according to others and create your own best way (a "my best way").

You Get What You Accept

The second common problem I've witnessed among people who are inauthentic is that they settle. The geniuses we studied don't settle. They are unreasonable in their expectations, regardless of what the culture says. They force life to work with them on their terms, not the other way around. They know what they are good at and what they like to do and they refuse to allow themselves to get into work or roles, or relationships for that matter, that force them to be unhappy being something they are not.

Just after college I went to work for Johnson & Johnson as a surgical sales representative. I was struggling as a sales person. It wasn't that I wasn't a good sales person, or that I wasn't smart or hard working enough, but that the sales process I had been taught wasn't a good fit for my natural drivers and talents. My motivations weren't the same as most of the other sales reps.

One day I was telling my sales manager, Rick Gilson, how unsatisfied I was with my own results. Rick told me something that day that seemed rather insignificant at the time, but later his words would take on a life of their own. Rick said, "You get what you accept."

When you really think about it, this disarmingly simple thought is actually one of the most powerful concepts you can own. It is the realization that you are in control, that you are the master of your own destiny, and this grand idea holds the power to set you free from any inauthenticity you have.

As Lao-Tzu put it in the famous *Tao Te Ching*, "Hold the great elephant (great idea) and the world moves." The concept of "you get what you accept" *is* the great elephant, and when you truly grasp this concept you realize that whatever your condition in life, you alone are ultimately responsible for how you deal with it. And this realization *should* move your world because it means that you just put yourself in the driver's seat.

Anthony Robbins, in *Awaken the Giant Within,* recalls the point in his life when he stopped accepting what he got. "I remember feeling like my life didn't matter, as if the events of the world were controlling me. I also remember the moment my life changed, the moment I finally said, 'I've had it! I know I'm much more than I'm demonstrating mentally, emotionally and physically in my life.' I made a decision in that moment which was to alter my life forever. I decided to change virtually every aspect of my life. I decided I would never again settle for less than I could be."

Not only is this a great example of someone who decided to stop accepting what he got, but it also shows the important shift from an external locus of control to an internal one. When Tony realized that he was in control of his success and destiny, his locus of control switched from believing that the world controlled him to believing that he controlled him. He realized he was in the driver's seat.

When you think about Rick Gilson's words, you realize that you are the only one who really can be responsible for your success. If you are the only one responsible for that success, and you don't have it, then you are the only one who can do anything about it. So, if you are unhappy with where you are in life, just remember, you get what you accept.

As for me, Rick's words will always play an important part in my life, but in some ways he probably regrets them, because when I did take them to heart I realized that I was being inauthentic, and once I decided to stop accepting that, I quit. It wasn't that Johnson & Johnson wasn't a great company to work for, they were. It wasn't that my role wasn't a valuable one, because it definitely was. It was just that I had allowed myself to take a job that did not let me be as authentic as I wanted to be.

I had allowed myself to take a job that didn't fully maximize my greatest natural talents, and once I realized I was the one who was responsible for this, I also realized that it was my responsibility to correct it. I owed it to myself. I left Johnson & Johnson and eventually started my own consulting firm, and now I get to be in the flow all day, every day. So thanks, Rick!

Geniuses absolutely refuse to settle, because they know they get what they accept. They accept only the best for themselves, and they get it.

A significant part of breaking that legacy of dependence means assuming full responsibility for your success, or lack thereof. It means becoming the boss of your own success.

A New Title

We all have many roles or titles in life (e.g. husband/wife, father/ mother, employee, friend, etc.), but in order to really take charge of your life, you need to add one more. That new title is what I call the SEO, or Self Executive Officer, which simply means that you will be the boss of your own life from now on.

Becoming your own SEO means taking charge of yourself for your own success. It means that while you may follow others (your boss, the crowd, etc.), you are ultimately the one responsible for your own success—no one else.

Michael Lorelli, the former President of PepsiCo East, talks about being your own SEO and taking charge of your own destiny when he describes the culture at PepsiCo. Michael says, "It was a cultural phrase at PepsiCo to say 'it's easier to ask for forgiveness than permission.' The culture supported being independent, taking risks and not looking to management to guide every action."

Being your own SEO means getting rid of your legacy of dependence, taking control of your own path to achieving your goals and doing what "feels" right, even if it isn't the traditional way.

An SEO Case Study: I knew a sales representative once named Rowan who was one of the most persuasive people I've ever known. When they say "he could sell ice to Eskimos," this is the guy they were talking about. As good as Rowan was at the actual art of selling, though, he absolutely stunk at being organized and seeing details. He wasn't lazy, and it wasn't a matter of attitude. According to the natural talent's profile I had given him, he had a blind spot for that kind of work. As a result, he was always missing his paperwork, constantly missing appointments or showing up without the proper equipment.

It was holding him back from succeeding in his role, so one day he decided to try to turn right instead of left. He asked his manager if he could get some relief in these areas by outsourcing some of his organizational duties to the sales manager's regional secretary.

For reasons that aren't important here, the manager said no, but it's what Rowan did next that is important. Instead of leaving his success in the hands of someone else, Rowan decided to take his success into his own hands and become his own SEO. Instead of saying, "I asked, oh well," he took that responsibility for himself and acted on his own.

Without asking his manager Rowan worked out a deal with another secretary in the office to help him with his organizational woes, in return for a small share of his commissions. Neither Rowan nor the secretary told management about any of this, but it worked out beautifully.

The point is that Rowan didn't allow his manager's poor decision to hinder his success. He found a way around his obstacles, and while he spent some of his own money to do it, it paid him a lot more in sales in the end.

Two years later, after his sales manager quit, Rowan let his new manager know all about the "unofficial" contract with the office secretary. The new, more enlightened, manager was able to see the value in the arrangement and the only change he insisted on was that his regional assistant take over the responsibilities instead of the office secretary and that she do this at the company's expense instead.

Regardless of whether or not Rowan followed directions or broke any rules (a legitimate topic for another discussion), he did take action to correct a problem that was inhibiting his success. He was freed up to focus on what he did best, was able to get in the flow much more often and ended up making a lot more money for himself and his employer. At the simplest level, what he did made him more authentic and made the company roughly $750,000 more in sales.

In *As Man Thinketh,* author James Allen views the issue of individual control over our own success in the following way: "The divinity that shapes our ends is in ourselves; it is our very self. And so we are held prisoner only by ourselves; our own thoughts and actions are the jailors of our fate—they imprison, if they are [untrue]; they also are the angels of freedom—they liberate, if they are [true]."

Think of a time when you knew that another route was the better way to go, but your company didn't agree. What did you do? Can you think of a time when you didn't become your own SEO and as a result, your success was limited? If you had gone ahead and done what you thought should be done, and it worked, what would the benefits have been versus the consequences of not having followed directions? The question to ask yourself is, "Am I my own jailor or angel?"

The exercise at the end of this section will take you through creating a job description for your new role as SEO.

The Above Average Trap

One of the things that many people tend to *accept* is the goal of becoming "above average." Many people actually set a goal to be considered above average. Being above average is safer than being the best. Being the best puts the spotlight on you, requires more bravery and often more self-honesty. For some—those who don't want to stand out—being above average allows them to feel good about themselves without having to be the best. Being above average is secure, whereas being great is always more tenuous (e.g. "Maybe next go round I won't be the best."). Being great requires that you challenge yourself, which is hard. Being mediocre and settling is easier.

The problem with being above average, though, is that it becomes a pair of padded handcuffs that hold you back and prevent you from becoming the genius you could be. Just like the leech that numbs you while it sucks your blood, being above average allows you to feel just fine with yourself while your true potential is drained right out of you. Be just average. Hell, be below average; at least that hurts enough that most people react to the pain and try to improve.

Being above average is that dangerous middle ground that isn't as painful as below average but not as hard and scary as being the best either. Its siren call can actually be very strong for a lot of people, and once you're there you can become so hypnotized that you lose all interest in anything else. Cover your ears and don't listen to that sweet, pain-free call of mediocrity. The most successful people among us don't accept mediocrity. They don't accept learned helplessness. They don't accept that they are flawed. They refuse to accept being just another runner in the race, and if they can't be the best, then they change races and find one where they can be. They seek out environments where their talents can make them the best, not just above average.

If you can't be the best in what you do—get the hell out! Do what Seth Godin talks about in his book, *The Dip*. Seth's advice: "Quit for all the right reasons." Don't waste your potential genius. Don't settle for anything less than what you deserve. Don't settle for being anything other than a genius at what you do.

> ~ *Being "above average" is to success what*
> *being "above ground" is to living.* ~

 Genius Action Step 2: Please log into your WYG Online workbook and complete the Pre-Evolution Exercises.

R | Chapter 6 Review

Chapter 1:
- "The Problem" is an epidemic of people that feel unfulfilled, dissatisfied and frustrated with their performance.

Chapter 2:
- To find out why, we created the Genius Project, and what we found were two key things:
  - There is no one "Genius Talent"; and
  - Self-Awareness and Authenticity are present in higher levels in the best performers.

Chapter 3:
- The myth of strengths and weaknesses supports our turning left instead of right.
- Geniuses turn right significantly more than they turn left.

Chapter 4:
- The effects of the problem go beyond performance issues to include negative physical and emotional effects.
- Inauthenticity causes you to feel upside down, always putting in more effort than you feel you get back in results, and blocks you from your passions and being in the flow.

Chapter 5:
- Today's organizations have shifted from an industrial to an intellectual economy.
- Legacy beliefs left over from the old industrial economy cause dependence and inauthenticity that damages individual performance.

Chapter 6:
- The first step in the solution is to prepare to change by deciding that:
  - You are in charge of your own success;
  - You get what you accept; and
  - You refuse to accept mediocrity.

CHAPTER 7

Revolution #1–
Know Thyself

"Know first who you are, and then adorn yourself accordingly."

~ EPICTETUS

"Gnothi Seauton"—Know Thyself. These words were inscribed above the entrance to the temple of Apollo at Delphi, the site of the sacred Oracle in Ancient Greece. People who visited the Oracle sought to find out what their destiny was or which course of action they should take in some particular matter. Ironically, though, those who entered seeking guidance failed to truly understand the real meaning of the message right above their heads. The message, "Know Thyself," didn't mean know for yourself—by asking someone else. It meant know of yourself as in "the answer lies within."

The best answers to your destiny lie within you and the only way to get those answers is to know your true talents by developing your own level of self-awareness. While you may have been created with certain talents, what you do with those talents is up to you. Your destiny is written by your own hand.

Self-Awareness

Aristotle said in the first line of *Metaphysics*, "Man, by nature, desires to know." The key to success, however, has a whole lot to do with *what* we know. The conventional belief on being successful focuses on having as much technical and factual knowledge as possible. A good lawyer must know the law, and a good scientist must know his or her science. While it is true that people need such knowledge to be good at what they do, the Genius Project highlighted another kind of knowledge—self-knowledge—as the key to being not just good, but great.

Self-knowledge involves a keen understanding and awareness of your own talents and non-talents. You are a wonderfully unique and singular mix of physical, emotional and spiritual content. You are your emotions, your experiences, your genetics and your dreams. As a matter of fact, there is so much to you that a definitive understanding of exactly who you are is just impossible. There is one aspect of who you are, however, that can be well understood, and that's your natural thinking style and talent.

Self-awareness is the first revolution in your journey to achieving your own 5th level of performance. People with higher levels of self-awareness take time to first learn, and then understand, their own natural thinking talents. They recognize the situations that will make them successful, and this makes it easy for them to find ways to achieve objectives that fit their talents. They also understand their limitations—where they are not effective—and this helps them understand where not to go and how not to be as well. Those who understand their natural talents are far more likely to pursue the right opportunities, in the right way, and get the results they desire.

> *"He who conquers himself is the greatest warrior of all."*
> ~ Confucious

How We Think

In order to become more aware of your natural thinking talents, you must become more aware of how your mind works, because it is your mind that creates your talents. And your mind is arguably the most miraculous creation in the entire universe. It controls every aspect of your life, conscious or subconscious. It never sleeps or stops gathering information.

Your mind is a remarkably effective CEO of a trillion-cell organization. It is voracious, taking in more than 11,000,000 bits of information every second of your life, and it has more processing capability than the most advanced computer ever built. In 2008, one of the fastest PC processor chips on the market was IBM's Power 6 at 4.7Ghz. The human brain is more like a 168Ghz chip.

It all starts at birth, when we are born with one hundred billion brain cells called neurons (100,000,000,000 cells or 10^{11}). That's more than any other creature on the planet. As we grow, each of these neurons reaches out and connects to other neurons to create what are called neural networks. By the time we are three years old each of our one hundred billion neurons has created a connection to approximately 15,000 other neurons, each of those having the same number of connections with other neurons.

Just imagine the incredible complexity of a network of living cells that large (think—1,500,000,000,000,000 or 1.5 quadrillion synaptic connections [1.5×10^{15}]). That's one million billion connections, and a whole lot of processing power. It is these networks that give us our ability to think, feel, remember, and be who we are.

Not all networks are created equally, though. Every time we have a recurring thought, or process information in a similar way, we use a similar network of neurons and that network becomes reinforced or more robust.

If you think of your brain as an organic internet connection, those conduits that are used more often are built into robust high-speed, high-bandwidth connections, while those that are not used fall into disrepair (atrophy) and become more like a dial-up connection than a cable modem. The high-speed connections can handle immense amounts of traffic, while the dial-up connections get choked and clogged with the smallest amount of data.

Travis Bradberry, in *The Personality Code,* describes them as "the conduits by which our brains think and the mental funnels through which our choices must flow." These neural networks eventually become mental filters that control which bits of information streaming into our brains get noticed, and which ones don't.

Throughout our early years, this continual process of creating and pruning neural networks forms permanent networks that will last our lifetimes, unchanged for the most part. And it is these neural networks that determine our natural talents for thinking and making decisions.

Because of the permanence of these neural networks, the natural talents they create are fixed. We cannot forcibly develop new neural networks through conscious effort in a weekend training program, thus we cannot develop new mental talents in the same way either.

This is what makes self-awareness such a vital aspect of your success. Since your natural mental talents are fixed, it is crucial that you understand what they are, because this is what you have to work with.

Geniuses, though, don't mind this fact. They don't sit around wishing that they could become something they are not. They revel in the fact that they have the special mix of talents they have because they embrace their uniqueness. We are all uniquely imperfect people, and this will never change nor should you want it to be any different.

How mind-numbingly boring would it be if we were all the same. Our uniqueness should be cherished and embraced. Success is not about ceasing to be uniquely imperfect or flawed. It is about finding your perfect match between your perfections and imperfections and what you do and how you do it.

> *"An unexamined life is a life not worth living."*
>
> ~ SOCRATES

One Brain—Two Minds

We may only have one brain, but it contains two different minds. The first mind, the one we are most familiar with, is the conscious mind. This is the logical, rational mind that we all consider when we think of *the mind,* because this is the mind we control. Intent is a key word for this mind because the results of the decisions we make with our conscious minds are *intentional*.

The second mind, however, operates well below the surface, or our awareness, making much more intuitive decisions without the intent seen in conscious thought. This is the mind we are more concerned with when we talk about self-awareness, and this is the mind you should be most interested in when it comes to improving your individual performance.

Even though this second mind (i.e. your subconscious mind) operates below the surface, that doesn't mean its effects are irrelevant or inconsequential. Quite the opposite! The effects that your subconscious mind has on your life are remarkable.

The jumbled paragraph below is a great example of how your subconscious mind can deliver results without your conscious mind's involvement or even awareness. Read the following paragraph as quickly as you can and see how easily it makes sense.

THE PAOMNNEHAL PWEOR OF THE HMUAN MNID. Aoccdrnig to a rscheearch at Cmabridge Uinervtisy, it deosn't mttaer in what order the ltteers in a word are, the only iprmoatnt thing is that the frist and lsat ltteer be in the rghit pclae. The rset can be a taotl mses and you can still raed it wouthit porbelm. This is bcuseae the sbucnsocoius mind deos not raed ervey lteter by istlef, but the word as a wlohe.

Could you read the words above? It was surprisingly easy, wasn't it? Actually, the faster you read the easier it probably was. That's because the faster you read, the more you relied on your subconscious mind. If you tried to use your conscious mind to do this it would take you much longer. Our subconscious minds can detect and pick up information up to 800 times faster than our conscious minds.

The subconscious mind, however, is capable of much more than simply helping us read faster. Without involving your conscious mind at all, your subconscious mind can give you super-human physical strength in emergencies by significantly increasing the hormones and blood that flow to your muscles. It can even slow down time, or at least your perception of it.

When not stressed or in danger, your brain is like a film projector operating at roughly thirty slides per second. In emergencies, though, the subconscious mind can more than double this processing speed, firing neurons more quickly. This increase in processing speed allows you to absorb and process more information in a fraction of the time, resulting in your perception that time has actually slowed down. It's very common to hear someone who has been in a car accident describe how an event that really only lasted seconds seemed to last much longer in his or her mind.

When our bodies are starving, the subconscious mind will kick in to promote our survival by changing our behavior, increasing our awareness and even urging us to eat things we normally would never consider eating.

Yachtsman Steve Callahan's boat sank in the open waters of the Atlantic Ocean in 1982. After his rations ran out, Steve started fishing to survive. After twenty-eight days of eating nothing but raw fish, he noticed his appetite for the fishes' meat decreasing. Instead he was craving parts of the fish he never would have normally considered edible.

The pure protein diet of flesh that Steve had been eating left his body depleted of crucial vitamins and water. Being aware of the vitamin deficiency and dehydration, Steve's subconscious mind released hormones like Orexin to increase his mental agility and coordination. It created cravings for other parts of the fish as well. Once Steve sampled parts like the skin (which contains Vitamin B) or the spine (which contains calcium and phosphates) or even the eyes (which contain fresh water), Steve's subconscious mind recognized their nutritional value and rewarded Steve by releasing endorphins that made them actually appealing.

In the end, thanks to his subconscious mind, Steve survived seventy-six days at sea without rations, and when rescued, he was actually in good physical health.

You don't have to be lost at sea to appreciate the powerful influence of your subconscious mind. Each night as you drift off to sleep, your subconscious mind causes the blood flow to your brain to nearly double its normal rate to support the extra diagnostic tune-ups that will be taking place. It even partially paralyzes your limbs so you won't act out your dreams.

Speaking of sleep, your subconscious mind never does. It is always processing the huge pile of stimuli that floods into your body through your senses, even while your conscious mind snoozes.

I personally experienced this aspect of my subconscious mind when I was in the military. During Desert Storm, I was assigned to a unit that served on a ready alert watch. This watch ran overnight so team members would try to get whatever sleep they could. However, even though our conscious minds were off in never-never land, there was always a part of our brains that was completely aware of our surroundings—that never turned off.

No matter how noisy it was, from trucks rumbling by to aircraft buzzing overhead, each of us was able to make ourselves fall asleep. The moment the ops phone (way on the other end of the hall) rang, though, each of us popped immediately out of bed. Normally, by the time the master at arms made it to the room to wake us, each of us was already awake and gearing up.

Our conscious minds may have been snoozing, but our subconscious minds were wide awake and attuned to that special sound. Parents who could sleep through a tornado but wake instantly to the slightest cry experience the same kind of subconscious attentiveness.

I could fill an entire book with similarly remarkable examples of the things the subconscious mind does to help us survive, but the key thing to understand is that not only does our subconscious mind play a significant part in helping us *survive* in life, it holds the greatest potential to help us *succeed* in life as well!

That's because it is your subconscious mind that influences and even controls the majority of the decisions you make every day. According to most studies, your subconscious mind is responsible for as much as 70% to 80% of the decisions you make. For this very reason, becoming a Genius, in our use of the term, means creating a life where you align what you are trying to do with the way your subconscious mind likes to think.

Just as your subconscious mind was surprisingly effective in reading the jumbled paragraph on page ninety-one, so too is your subconscious mind surprisingly effective when it comes to your natural talents. That's the whole key to reaching the 5th level of performance and becoming a genius at something. When you learn to trust your subconscious mind, and manage to create a role where everything you do aligns well with your subconscious thinking talents, the results you get will be much more efficient and accurate, even though they require less effort.

Subconscious Mind Exercise

Here's another little demonstration of the fact that even though you forget it, your subconscious mind is always working behind the scenes to influence or even control what you do in the real world. While seated, take your dominant leg and raise it off the seat but keep your foot hanging down free and loose. Now start to rotate that foot in a clockwise circle. Nothing too grand, just say a 12-inch circle. Now, at the same time, take your dominant hand and place it in the air in front of you like you were writing on an invisible black board. While continuing to rotate your foot in the same clockwise direction, use your finger to draw a 12-inch letter "S" on the invisible board in front of you. Go ahead and draw that letter S now. What happened with your foot when you drew the letter S? For the vast majority of you, your foot started following your hand and began to move counter clockwise. Why? You didn't consciously tell your leg to start going in the opposite direction did you? It happened because your subconscious mind has developed such a strong habit for thinking that the direction of an S is counter clockwise, and your conscious mind was overridden and both limbs listened to your subconscious mind.

You may have trouble actually hearing your subconscious mind, but it is there. Your body heard it even if your conscious mind did not.

The problem with the subconscious mind, however, is that we don't trust it. We are suspicious of it. We live in a world that assumes that the quality of the decisions we make are directly related to the time and effort we put into them.

Doctors put lots of conscious effort into every decision—don't they? The best managers carefully weight all the pros and cons before acting—right? And what are we taught about making decisions? Haste makes waste. Look before you leap. Stop and think. Don't judge a book by its cover. We are taught that the more information we gather, and the more carefully we deliberate, the more accurate our decision will be.

This view assumes that when we are at our decision-making best, we are the pride and joy of Plato, Descartes and Kant (all of whom argued that rational reasoning and logic deliver the best decisions). The subconscious mind, however, has much more to do with controlling our decisions than we give it credit.

One of the reasons experts think the subconscious even exists is because our conscious mind has a very limited capacity. To survive in the world, people must be able to process a great deal of information, more than we can consciously juggle at one time. It all comes down to efficiency.

According to author and brain-researcher Dr. Timothy Wilson,

> Scientists have tried to determine how many of these signals can be processed consciously at any given point in time. The most liberal estimate is that people can process consciously about forty pieces of information every second. Think about it; we can take in 11,000,000 pieces of information a second, but can only process forty of them consciously. What happened to the other 10,999,960? It would be terribly wasteful to design a system with such incredible sensory acuity but very little capacity to use the incoming information. Fortunately, we do make use of a great deal of this information outside of conscious awareness.

Our subconscious mind tends to get involved more in the smaller decisions than in the larger ones. Deciding to close down an entire division is not only a decision that will most likely be made using conscious thought, but also one that will probably be better served as a result.

My focus in this book is on the thousands, or tens of thousands, of small subconscious decisions you make every day. These have a much greater impact on your personal performance than do the few and infrequent big decisions you make.

The Father of the Genius Profile

When it comes to understanding how we make these subconscious decisions, we've come a long way since 440BC when Greek physician Hippocrates first documented a formal understanding of traits in how we think. Hippocrates called them the Humors. Fast forward some 2,000 years to the early 1900s, when psychologists like Carl Jung and William Marston made significant advances by defining their own universal models of behavior. Edward Spranger and Gordon Allport also added to our understanding by defining new motivational models. Countless others have added their pieces to this understanding since then, but in 1963, a German immigrant by the name of Robert Hartman introduced work that raised our understanding of how we think and make decisions to a whole new level.

As a young boy in Berlin, Germany, in 1917, Robert Hartman would stand with the rest of his classmates and recite an oath under Kaiser Wilhelm II, which included the phrase, "I was born to die for Mother Germany." From an early age Robert believed this oath was wrong, and he would grow to have significant differences of opinion with many of his countrymen on the sanctity and value of human life.

Hartman witnessed the rise of the Nazi party, and the evil they seemed to be powered by, and this spurred him to dedicate his entire life to the study of "what is good." His journey to understand how people perceive what is good would lead him to understand how we perceive anything. Eventually, this led to his creation of Formal Axiology, the science of how we perceive ourselves and the world around us. In no small way, Dr. Hartman's work is the impetus behind this book.

Eventually Hartman fled persecution in Germany to the United States where he taught at several universities, including Yale and MIT. He conducted research with Timothy Leary at Harvard and collaborated with Abraham Maslow on his famous Hierarchy of Needs. Under Dr. Hartman's guidance, his insight into the infinite value of the individual would fuel the creation of the first Profit Sharing Commission in the United States in the 1940s. This council would be one of the first to challenge the Industrial era's view on the value of the individual, and out of that work would eventually grow the 401K retirement plan we know today.

Dr. Robert S. Hartman's impact on our modern world was significant to say the least. His life's work eventually earned him a nomination for the Nobel Peace Prize in 1973, an award many believe he would have won had he not passed away two weeks later, since prizes were not awarded posthumously.

It is due to his work, and those who fought to make sure his work survived him, that we can all now achieve a higher level of self-awareness and appreciation for the "good" in all of us. Dr. Hartman's work led to the creation of the profile we used in the Genius Study, the genius profile you will take in this book and the model we'll use to define your natural mental talents—starting now.

The Head, Hand and Heart

The root of Dr. Hartman's discovery was in his identification of three distinct dimensions of value (i.e. different ways of judging or evaluating any situation or thing). All of the natural thinking talents you have fit into one of these three core categories or *classes of talent*.

Though I've revised Hartman's original titles to make them more contemporary and easier to understand for our consulting clients, his three classes of talent are:

- The Head (Hartman's Systemic): the class of talents that deals with intellectual or conceptual thinking, creating order and structure, long-range planning, problem solving, and big-picture or strategic thinking. This class of talents is sometimes referred to as *Thinking*.
- The Hand (Hartman's Extrinsic): the class of talents that deals with practical thinking, real-world action orientation, details,

results, and tangible or tactical thinking. This class of talents
is sometimes referred to as *Doing*.
- The Heart (Hartman's Intrinsic): the class of talents that deals
with people, empathy, sensitivity and understanding for others
and emotional or humanistic thinking. Sometimes this class of
talents is known as *Feeling*.

While all of us possess some level of ability in all three of these
classes, they are not all equal. All of that creating and pruning of
neural networks that each of us went through early on in life caused
us to develop our own unique levels of ability in each class of talent.
   For example:

- Some people have a natural talent for the Head dimension,
and as such they possess superior talents for intellectualizing,
theorizing, solving complex problems and thinking strategically;
- Some people have more robust neural networks for dealing
with the Hand dimension and find they have natural talents
for understand how things work, being able to stay locked onto
the goal without distraction, being pragmatic and thinking
tactically; and
- Still others find their greatest set of talents in the Heart dimension; they are naturally gifted when it comes to understanding
others, being aware of their thoughts and emotions, communicating with them, perceiving their motivations and connecting
with them.

I like to use three figures from my childhood to help illustrate
the differences in these three classes of talent.
   In the early seventies, reruns of Star Trek were a regular part of
daily life for many kids my age. In the TV series, actors William
Shatner played Captain James Tiberius Kirk, Leonard Nimoy was Mr.
Spock, and DeForest Kelley played the role of Dr. Leonard "Bones"
McCoy. If you are familiar with the characters, you might recognize
the three classes of talent right off the bat:

- Mr. Spoc, the science officer, is an ideal proxy for the Head dimension, always very logical, very theoretical, structured, and constantly *thinking* more than feeling or doing;
- Captain Kirk makes a great representative for the Hand dimension as the person who is forever focused on the tactical situation, much more pragmatic and focused on *doing* more than thinking or feeling; and
- Finally there is Bones, the ship's physician, who is an ideal representative for the Heart dimension; Bones was always focused on the people, trying to balance the needs of the mission with the needs of the people, and forever running afoul of his logical or practical peers in favor of human need; Bones was more about *feeling* than thinking or doing.

While it's possible to have equal levels of natural talent in each dimension, most people develop varying levels and ability in each, and it is this combination that makes each of us unique.

Masters and Blind Spots

Just as all neural networks are not created equally, so, too, are all classes of talent not equal. The more robust the network, the clearer you see that aspect of reality. The less developed the network, the more ambiguous that aspect of reality will seem to you. It is different for each person. One person's mind might see the factual aspect of a situation and be blind to the humanistic aspects, so while they make sure action is taken, they are blind to the fact that in doing so they have irritated a lot of people. Another person might see the humanistic aspects of the situation very clearly, but completely miss the big picture, so even though the bus is headed in completely the wrong direction, at least everyone on the bus is feeling valued and understood.

I describe the stronger networks or classes of talent as *masters* and the less developed ones as potential *blind spots*. Master dimensions are more developed and efficient, and you won't likely ignore these aspects of reality. On the other hand, blind-spot dimensions are not as dominant, and you may sometimes ignore this aspect of reality.

Your varying level of ability in these classes of talent is what creates the talents and non-talents that you must become well aware of if you want to reach your 5th level of performance.

Ready to learn what your level of talents in these areas is and meet your own Genius? Please go to your online workbook and complete Genius Action Step # 3 (i.e. take the Genius Profile).

> **(G) Genius Action Step 3:** Please log into your WYG Online workbook and complete the Genius Profile.

Meet Your Genius

> *"Most people live in a very restricted circle of their*
> *potential being. We all have reservoirs of energy and*
> *genius to draw upon of which we do not dream."*
>
> ~ WILLIAM JAMES

Now that you have completed your own Genius Profile, let's walk you through your results so you can get a better understanding of your talents.

Before we do that, however, let's address the most common question we hear with this profile. The question is an important one, because without believing the results of your profile, you won't be able to benefit from the information and insight it provides.

That question often goes something like this: "How can you get anything valuable out of such a short and seemingly nonsensical ordering of a bunch of disconnected statements?" While the profile you just took is based on over fifty years of research, has been validated numerous times over many years, and used with hundreds of thousands of individuals around the world, it does seem incredibly easy for some. One reason for this is because it is measuring your subconscious decision-making process.

Unlike most other instruments, the Genius Profile is not asking you for your conscious opinion. Just like you were probably surprised at how easy it was to read that jumbled text from the Cambridge paragraph, so, too, does the instrument seem surprisingly easy, because it is your subconscious mind doing all the work, not your conscious mind.

The Report

I usually recommend that people read through the results more than once and then observe their lives with an objective eye to truly consider what it says and how they see it manifested in their daily lives. Your report is likely to give you information that is a little surprising and often takes objectivity to grasp. Being truly objective is a hard thing to do so it doesn't hurt to ask others how accurate they think the results are.

When you look at the results of your Genius Profile objectively and openly, and when you are reintroduced to your inner genius, it can be a wonderful experience. I say "reintroduced," because this genius has always been inside you. You knew it well when you were a pure and innocent child who didn't give any thought to what you should be, or how you should be. You approached the world from your own unique perspective then, without much thought for whether it was correct or not.

In the book, *Surrounded By Geniuses,* author Allan Gregerman describes our perception as children like this:

> When we were kids, we saw things differently. We didn't have preconceived notions about ourselves or the world around us. Every day we engaged the world authentically, with passion, energy, fresh eyes and a compelling sense of wonder, curiosity and, most importantly, honesty. But somewhere between childhood and the world of adult work, most of us lost this knack for seeing ourselves and the world around us as a rich soil for unlocking new ideas and opportunities. As we grew older, we began to see ourselves and others for what they appeared to be rather than what they could be. We began to see things and even ideas for what they appeared to be in the context in which we found them, rather than what they could be in a new context that we could create for them.

Your task in this chapter is to take an open and objective view of your results and what they tell you about yourself. While doing that, ask yourself how familiar this feels, how much you recognize this genius hiding within. How long has it been since you spoke with this genius? How good and faithful a friend have you been to it over the years?

You might think of it as something that was precious and cherished when you were a child, but then you grew up and it got stored away with other childhood mementos in a box hiding in your attic. You completely forgot all about it, but now, upon rediscovering it, your memories of how this genius served you come flooding back, and you want to show it to those you love ("Hey, look what I found!"). This chapter will reintroduce you to your genius, and the rest of the book will teach you how to use this genius to become more authentic and successful.

Now let's walk through the report and break out each section to explain its content.

Pages 1–3

The cover of your report contains a symbol for your unique Genius pattern. We'll expand on this later in the report. The next three pages of your Genius Profile are basically introductory text. This information gives you some additional background on the three classes of talent being measured.

Page 4

Page four of your profile is where you will start to see information that is specific to you only. This page gives you an overall understanding of your specific Genius pattern. It deals with how developed each of your three classes of talents is and what your preference is for using them.

Underneath the pattern title, you'll also see which of the classes of talents are your masters and which are your blind spots. Let me stress here that just because something is listed as a "blind spot," that doesn't mean you have *no* ability or talent in that area—it is just that relative to your master dimensions, these blind spots are less developed—enough so that when you are making subconscious decisions, you may miss these things, and they can become a blind spot. Since, as we discussed earlier, as much as 80% of the decisions you make on any given day are subconsciously driven, it's important that you understand your masters and blind spots as well as you can, because it is this knowledge that you must leverage for optimal performance.

Underneath the general pattern overview is a "motto" meant to represent your Genius pattern in a very simplified form. While not at all fully representative, it captures the overall Gestalt of your natural thinking talents.

Page 5

On page five of your genius report, you'll find two lists. The first one contains some potential strengths that could be realized by depending on your natural talents. Remember, these are listed as potential strengths, because they can only become strengths when you rely on your natural talents. The second list contains specific attributes associated with your unique genius pattern. These are actual mental talents you can leverage for greater success.

> **Action Step:** As you look at the items on page five, ask yourself how much your success currently depends on these things. Take a moment to draw a circle around those things on the page that you feel your current job or role depends heavily on. Did you circle all the potential strengths and talents or only some? If you didn't circle all of them, then you might not be maximizing your talents for optimal performance. You might be leaving talents as unrealized potential strengths. In the next chapter, you will learn how to increase your dependence on any talents you didn't circle, so you can become even more authentic.

Also on page five is a short description called your "Results Drive," which is a summary statement of how you prefer to achieve results. Depending on your masters, you might seek to achieve results primarily through creating systems and structure (master for the Head dimension), or by action and doing things yourself (master for the Hand), or through others (master for the Heart)—or any combination thereof.

Action Step: Look at your results drive and ask yourself if you are currently trying to achieve results in this or some other way. Is this the primary way you seek to achieve results, is it just one of the ways, or is it not a way in which you seek to get results at all? If your primary way of achieving results in life is very close to your Results Drive in your Genius Profile, you are being authentic in this one aspect. If it is only one of several ways in which you attempt to achieve results, or not your way at all, then this is another area where you are being inauthentic, and something we will address in the next chapter.

Page 6

On page six of your genius report, you'll find specific examples of your non-talents and potential weaknesses. Remember, just like the potential strengths on page five, these are listed as potential weaknesses, because they can only become weaknesses if you depend on your non-talents.

Action Step: Just as you did with the talents and potential strengths on page five, look at the list of specific non-talents on page six and ask yourself how much your success currently depends on each. Take a moment to draw a circle around those things that your job currently depends heavily on. Did you circle any of the non-talents or potential weaknesses or only some? If you didn't circle any of them, then you are very authentic in your role, because it doesn't require you to rely on non-talents. If you did circle anything on page six you are allowing your success to depend on these non-talents, which causes you to be inauthentic. In Chapter Eight, I'll show you how to remove your dependence on these non-talents and convert them from real weaknesses back to only potential weaknesses.

Page 7

Page seven of your genius profile contains an easy-to-use reference chart called the Performance Focus Chart. I recommend you print this chart out and post it somewhere where you can refer to it frequently. Eventually, it would be best if you memorized this chart. This guide is designed to help you make decisions that are more authentic for your natural talents. Look at each class of talents, and if it is a master for you, follow the guidance in the first column. If a class of talents is a blind spot for you, simply follow the guidance in the second column.

For example, John has the Efficient pattern, so he has masters in the Head and Hand dimensions, but a blind spot in the Heart dimension. When John looks at the Performance Focus chart below, he can be reminded to take clues from the top right section.

G	Performance Focus	
	If Master	If Blind Spot
Heart	*Remember to* • Consider others' thoughts • Ask others' opinions • Listen to others' needs • Involve and depend on others	*Avoid having to* • Be very empathetic • Share performance with a team • Get results "through" others
Hand	*Remember to* • Pay attention to details • Act—pull the trigger • Move—stop thinking or talking	*Avoid having to* • Be very detail oriented • Be tactical • Perform repetitive/detailed tasks
Head	*Remember to* • See the big picture • Stop and think • Plan far ahead • Create a process to follow	*Avoid having to* • Be very strategic • Solve complex theoretical problems • Work within rigid structured environments

In John's specific case, he would want to remember to focus on the details, take action and keep moving, while also paying attention to the big picture, planning accordingly and creating a process to follow. Since he has a blind spot for the Heart dimension, however, he would benefit from remembering to avoid having to be very empathetic, sharing his performance with a team of others, or getting results through others.

Use the guide on the previous page to help you maintain a focus on where your talents are.

Page 8

On page eight of your genius profile, you'll find another chart that is meant to give you some simple rules to follow to help you maximize your talents and minimize your non-talents. This chart will help you decide when you need to slow down and think more consciously (because you are dealing with a non-talent), or when you can let your subconscious mind rule the day (because you are dealing with a talent). I recommend you print this chart out as well and become very familiar with it, because it can provide you with some very simple insights into how to change your approach in what you do.

My Decision-Making Action Rules

Your Talents	Your Blind Spots
Speed Up When you are involved in a strength activity, feel free to speed up. You don't have to think about it too much, or consciously reason through as much. You can rely on your subconscious mind and react knowing that all your natural talents are behind you.	**Slow Down** When you are involved in a blind spot area (2nd and 3rd place preferences), slow down a little, think things through a little more, and use more of your conscious reasoning than simply reacting.
Take the Lead When you face a situation involving your area of strength, feel free to take more of a lead in any group setting, to lead the way toward what needs to be done.	**Follow** When you face a situation involving your blind spot areas, you may want to follow someone else's lead who has a strength in that aspect of a situation.
Trust When dealing with an area of strength for you, trust your gut, and go with your first thought.	**Question** When dealing with a blind spot area, question your gut a little bit. Don't just go with it blindly without taking a second look at your first thought.

Sticking with the example of John, whenever he finds himself dealing with a task that involves talents associated with the Head or Hand dimensions he can: speed up, take the lead and trust his gut. If, however, he finds himself dealing with people issues, because he knows that this is a blind spot for him, he can use this chart to help him remember to: slow down, follow the lead of others who are more talented in this area, and question his initial gut instinct, as it might not be as accurate.

By utilizing these action steps, you can learn either to let your subconscious mind run free or to rein it in and start thinking with your conscious mind.

Go ahead and review your Genius Profile from beginning to end and become familiar with the talents, non-talents, potential strengths and weaknesses and the two charts. This information can be used to start changing how you get results immediately.

Master Patterns

Patterns are a common and easy way to understand how multiple variables play together. When we do this with the three classes of talents, we come up with seven unique patterns (or Master Patterns). An expanded definition for each of the Master Patterns can be found in Appendix B.

The seven Master Patterns are:
1. The Balanced Pattern—Masters: Head, Hand & Heart. Blind Spot: none
2. The Social Pattern—Masters: Hand & Heart. Blind Spot: Head
3. The Director Pattern—Masters: Head & Heart. Blind Spot: Hand
4. The Efficient Pattern—Masters: Head & Hand. Blind Spot: Heart
5. The Supportive Pattern—Master: Heart. Blind Spots: Hand & Head

6. The Practical Pattern—Master: Hand. Blind Spots: Head & Heart
7. The Systematic Pattern—Master: Head. Blind Spots: Heart & Hand

The chart below gives you a visual understanding of how these three classes of talents can be mixed to create these seven combinations or patterns. Dark boxes with "√" represent the class of talent that are your *masters*. Those boxes in white represent dimensions that can become your *blind spots* and create areas where information is missed or not factored into your decisions.

	Classes of Talents			
Pattern Title	Head (Systems)	Hand (Tasks)	Heart (People)	*My Masters*
Balanced	√	√	√	Systems & Tasks & People
Social		√	√	Tasks & People
Director	√		√	Systems & People
Efficient	√	√		Systems & Tasks
Supportive			√	People
Practical		√		Tasks
Systematic	√			Systems

To help flesh these patterns out, I've pulled some real-life examples from the geniuses interviewed for this book to represent their own specific patterns. Find your own Genius pattern and see if you can see some of yourself in what these geniuses have to say about their own patterns.

Anthony Robbins
(Pattern #1. The Balanced Genius Pattern)

Masters: Head/Hand/Heart.
Blind Spots: None

Tony is a classic example of someone who possesses equally high levels of ability in all three classes of talents. None of his dimensions are more developed than any other, so technically his pattern has three masters. As a result, he has no blind spots. The number one trait for the Balanced pattern is a feeling of "conflict" in that if at any given moment you are focusing on one master, you feel as if you are ignoring the other two. While Balanced patterns make very objective and sound decisions, they also feel they should be living in all three places at the same time. You can think of it like a mother of triplets who feels guilty whenever she is caring for just one of her children at a time. In other words, people with the Balanced pattern beat themselves up more than any other pattern because they are always trying to serve three masters (e.g. see the big strategic picture, while focusing on the tactical aspects, *and* being people oriented all the while). Tony is constantly struggling with this issue. Not only does he drive himself incredibly hard, which *has* been a great benefit to him, but in so doing he can sometimes wear out anyone around him. While he has natural talents in all three classes, if those around him do not possess equal ability, they can easily become exhausted trying to cover all the angles that Tony does. This pattern also supports Tony's success by helping him take the big picture and find a way to make it understandable to all kinds of people. His passion for life is so very well captured in this pattern (i.e. Help others [heart] understand themselves better [head] and apply that knowledge to improve their lives in significant ways [hand]). This pattern's motto captures the emphasis on all three masters, "It's important to think about it, and talk about it, but you've got to also get it done as well."

Dan Lyons
(Pattern #2. The Social Genius Pattern)
Masters: Hand/Heart.
Blind Spots: Head

Dan has the Social Pattern, which tends to place more importance, and see more clearly, the Hand and Heart dimensions. This pattern is more about deciding what needs to be done and eliciting others to achieve those results. As such, Dan is someone who tends to see the practical realities, and the people around him, as being more important than following some previously set, possibly outdated, strategic view or rigid set of policies or structure. While structure, theory and strategy are important, figuring out how to make things work right now, and getting those results with or through others, is a more important concern to Dan or anyone else with this pattern. This pattern often supports people in team settings that are very dynamic or fluid. Oftentimes, following a prescribed set of policies or structure is not as important as delivering real-world results, which may require changing the established procedure or policy. What makes sense theoretically may not make sense practically to this pattern. When we talk about the blind spot for this pattern (i.e. the Head), we are not saying that people with this pattern can't live in their heads and be strategic, create structure and follow an orderly process—just that if left to their own druthers, they naturally tend to focus less on creating a plan for everything and concentrate more on working with what they've got and who is around to get it done. This can cause someone with this pattern to become more of an *ad hoc* person, favoring a pragmatic approach that incorporates a solid understanding of others with a realist's approach to what must be done to achieve results. This pattern's motto captures the emphasis on the Hand and Heart masters: "Don't over-think it, just get everyone on board, and let's go do it."

Garry Titterton
(Pattern #3. The Director Genius Pattern)

Masters: Head/Heart.
Blind Spots: Hand

Garry is a good example of the Director pattern, which has masters for the Head and Heart classes of talent. This pattern finds the greater levels of talent in the Head and the Heart. In other words, people with this pattern have natural talents for: theoretical thinking, big-picture understanding, complex problem-solving and long-range planning. They are also naturally good at understanding others and merging their strategic talents with their emotional ones—resulting in what typically becomes strategic leadership (i.e. determining a path and getting results through others). As such, Garry, and others who share this pattern with him, is very good at seeing the big strategic picture and understanding how others fit into that image. He is naturally adept at seeing the long-range plan for what needs to take place to achieve results, and who he has available to achieve those results through. In many leadership roles, this pattern helps create a person who naturally tends to think about the overall strategic vision and how to get it through people. These people enjoy a structured approach to things instead of an *ad hoc*, or seat-of-the-pants, kind of approach. One con of this pattern is that being somewhat less concerned with the Hand dimension, it might lead someone to lose sight of the details of a situation, even to ignore them, considering them minutia or a distraction. Garry explains how when he allows himself to get sucked into thinking too much about the details, he doesn't perform as well, because this is neither where his talents lie, or where he enjoys being. He likes to stay in the balloon at an altitude that allows him to work on the big picture and orchestrate the activities of others. This pattern's motto captures the emphasis on Head and Heart masters: "Stop to think and talk about it sufficiently before proceeding."

Rosemary Hygate (Pattern #4. The Efficient Genius Pattern)

Masters: Head/Hand. Blind Spots: Heart

Rosemary Hygate, or Rosie as she prefers, is a great example of the Efficient genius pattern. As one of the best executive assistants in Hollywood for a long time, Rosie applies her genius to bring order and stability to the chaotic lives of the movie stars she works for. Her upbringing in an all-girls boarding school outside London instilled in her a strong belief for order, structure and results and it is these qualities that her employers appreciate so very much. The biggest value Rosie brings to the stars she works for is her ability to organize their crazy and hectic lives. She is able to divine an order out of the chaos that is their schedules, and help them retain some semblance of sanity and organization in their lives. More than simply assisting around the house, Rosie has benefited her employers with her genius for organizing and delivering structured results by helping with public relations, organizing schedules and charity events, all aspects of public exposure, payroll management—even managing an Arabian horse farm for one celebrity actor. Many might assume that the Heart dimension would be most important in the role of executive assistant, but the stars Rosie works for have plenty of people to love them and nurture them. What they really need is someone to keep them organized. Rosie's masters in the Head and Hand allow her to do just that. She is able to see the big picture, identify the crucial aspects or key components of a situation, and create processes, order, and structure to what is normally a cluttered mess. "She keeps me sane, my life is a wreck without her" said one of her most recent employers. Rosie is also a great example of how you can be a genius at anything. Rosie isn't the CEO of a multi-national company, nor one of the movie stars that she helps live a more sane life. She is, however, living proof that anything that can be done can be done at genius levels. If you ask around Hollywood you will find that Rosemary Hygate, as one of the best executive assistants in Hollywood, is truly considered a genius at what she does.

This pattern's motto captures the emphasis on the Head and Hand masters: "Make sure to think it through, and then make it happen, no time to talk about it."

Laurence Higgins
(Pattern #5. The Supportive Genius Pattern)
Masters: Heart.
Blind Spots: Head/Hand

To some, Dr. Laurence Higgins might be a somewhat surprising choice to represent the Supportive pattern. This pattern indicates a strength in the class of talents that has to do with people—understanding them, motivating them, getting results through them and very accurately reading the subtle signs of their thoughts, needs, fears and emotions. The Supportive pattern excels in communicating with others, resolving conflict and understanding people so clearly that sometimes they have a better sense for what people should do than the individuals themselves. This pattern has its cons as well, though. People with this pattern tend to struggle with being very well organized on a practical level. Creating lots of structure and policies is another area where people with this pattern do not easily excel. People with supportive patterns tend to place much more importance on understanding people than they do on having lots of rules and processes. Most people might assume that one of the top orthopedic surgeons in the world would be all about the Head and the Hand. Dr. Higgins' true genius, though, is for understanding others. Being acutely attuned to the emotional mind-sets of his patients, Dr. Higgins actually talks more patients out of surgery than he talks into it. There is a large body of evidence that shows that a person's mental attitude plays a significant role in how successful the outcome of his or her surgery or treatment will be, and his genius allows him to be a great judge of whether or not someone is really ready for surgery from a mental or emotional state. He cites this as one of the biggest reasons for his success as a surgeon and his success rate with his patients. This pattern's motto captures the emphasis on the Heart master: "I need to know how everyone feels before I can decide what needs to be done and how."

Michael Lorelli
(Pattern #6. The Practical Genius Pattern)
Masters: Hand.
Blind Spots: Head/Heart

The Practical pattern is just that—practical. Above all else—whether other's thoughts or opinions, compliance with established rules, or the long-range plan—this pattern excels in one class of talents, and that is making things happen—now. The practical pattern has at its center the class of talents associated with the Hand. Unlike the Head, which deals with intellectual things, or the Heart, which deals with the humanistic world, the Hand deals with real-world, pragmatic, goal-focused and action-oriented results. If the Head translates to "thinking about it," and the Heart translates to "understanding others," the Hand translates to "just do it." People with this pattern are typically prone to action without overly drawn-out strategies and planning. They become jazz musicians who improvise, depending on what the world throws at them, to get results. Sometimes this focus can cause them to not focus as much on the people involved. It can also cause them to focus less on creating elaborate structures or reproducible procedures (choosing often to "wing-it" instead). Michael Lorelli is a great example of the Practical pattern, and is someone whose successes have centered around his willingness to break with the accepted program, bend the rules where he felt they needed bending and see the most practical route to achieving his goals based on what the world gives him. One con to this pattern is that sometimes results come at the expense of the rules or others, but Michael is quick to recount his favorite saying at one of his last companies, "It's better to ask for forgiveness than permission." From being the first ever to advertise on the sails of an America's Cup sailboat to the first to place an advertisement in a rented home movie, Michael's genius has been his ability always to see the practical route and not be distracted by what others think he *should* do, or what the rules say he *can't* do. This pattern's motto captures the emphasis on the Hand master: "Stop thinking and talking about it—Just Do It!"

Marshall Goldsmith (Pattern #7. The Systematic Genius Pattern)

Masters: Head. Blind Spots: Hand/Heart

The Systematic pattern is a process builder. People with the greatest class of talents associated with the Head dimension are exquisite big-picture people and creators of systems. They often start by being the one who sees the obvious simple truth in a complex process or system. They excel at being able to see the big picture and identifying what is and isn't working among all the moving parts. This is something that those who don't share this genius may have a very hard time seeing with as much clarity or ease. People with a single master for the Head can look at a very complicated situation and distill it down to its simplest essence, highlighting the relevant facts and relegating the non-essential elements to a corner somewhere out of the way. This helps make them great at figuring out what the problem is first and then creating a solution that is reproducible, complete and understandable. People with this pattern are also very good at teaching others how to understand difficult or complex concepts, because they have such a grasp of the whole system in their heads that they can compartmentalize it into more easily understood bits. One area where people with this pattern aren't as strong is in being very attentive to the fine details from a practical point of view, or being overly sensitive to other people's emotions. Dr. Goldsmith has a Systematic pattern, and he has taken his genius in this area and built an incredibly successful reputation as the go-to guy whom you want helping you figure out how to get to the next level of performance. As an executive coach who works with already successful people to make them even more successful, Marshall has a talent for taking very complex concepts and turning them into easy-to-understand lessons that anyone can grasp. The lessons he creates are designed to highlight client behaviors that to him might seem rather obvious, but are often something his clients are blind to. His slight blind spot to the emotional dimension (the Heart dimension) actually helps him do this, because he is very good at giving people very negative information about themselves without, to quote him directly, "getting caught up in turning that into an emotional situation." He keeps such discussions very rational and unemotional. This pattern's motto captures the emphasis on the Head master: "Think it through."

Reason Versus Reaction

> *"Intuition will tell the thinking mind where to look next."*
>
> ~ DR. JONAS SALK

Intuition: *knowledge from within; instinctive knowledge or feeling without the use of rational processes"* Oxford English Dictionary

In addition to actually measuring your natural talents, one of the best ways you can learn to start using your natural talents is simply to listen to them more.

You see, the voices in your head never stop speaking to you, and even though you may have become quite adept at ignoring them, they are still there, talking to you all the time—you just don't realize it.

They are seen on the surface as what is typically called intuition, and this is what you must learn to listen to better if you are going to reach your own level of genius performance.

Intuition is *not* about extrasensory perception (ESP), a sixth sense or anything mystical or metaphysical. It *is* about data, gathered by your five senses, being recognized by your subconscious mind instead of your conscious mind.

Carl Jung noted, "Intuition does not denote something contrary to reason, but something outside of the province of reason." Intuition is about instinctive or subconscious awareness. When I talk with people about the difference between using their conscious and subconscious minds, I use the words *reasoning* and *reacting*. Reasoning is the result of logical, rational thought driven by the conscious mind. Reacting is the result of following the intuitive, subconscious mind.

Since the subconscious mind misses nothing and is aware of everything around you, whenever you have a feeling about something you can't explain, it is usually the case that you just can't explain it based on what your conscious mind is aware of.

Intuition is that sudden flash of insight that comes out of nowhere. It's that sense you get or decision you make without really thinking about it; it just comes to you. In reality, it doesn't come out of nowhere. It comes from everything your subconscious mind is aware of.

Instead of dismissing intuition as an unfounded and irrational impulse, reaching the 5th level of performance requires that you learn to accept and respect this voice, as it is your natural talents talking to you.

This is easier said than done, though. Just as we are taught not to trust our subconscious mind as much as our conscious one, we're also taught to go with what we know, not what we feel.

> *"The intuitive mind is a sacred gift and the rational*
> *mind a faithful servant. We have created a society that*
> *honors the servant and has forgotten the gift."*
> ~ ALBERT EINSTEIN

Of mammals, humans seem to be the only ones that actively discourage listening to intuition, but there is a lot of research that proves that intuition actually plays a larger role in decision-making than most conventional teaching would lead us to believe.

- Research into the decision-making of consumers shows that as much as 95% of the decision to purchase something is subconscious (Harvard-Zaltman, 2003).
- Research on fire fighters showed that 80% of their decisions were subconscious and intuitive rather than logical and rational (Klein et al., 2003).
- Research on naval commanders showed that 95% of their decisions were based on intuition and "gut" rather than actually analyzing and comparing options (Klein et al., 1996).
- Yet another study of commercial airline crews in 1991 found that more than 95% of their decisions were what was termed "snap judgments," which are those based on intuition, not rationale (Mosier, 1991).
- In a study of offshore oilfield managers, one study showed similarly that 90% of their decisions were not of the conscious,

rational type, rather they were snap judgments and intuitive (Flin, 1996).

Great athletes are often quoted as saying, "If I have to *think* about it, it's too late." Even those people that most of us would assume must be very logical and rational turn out to be very much driven by their intuitions.

Physicist Albert Einstein's genius for conceptual thinking was much more a feeling for him than a rationalization of the facts. So intuitive and pure was this talent, that he only vaguely understood it and rarely attempted to use words or logic to define it. In his work, *Principles of Research,* Einstein said, "There is no logical path to [truth]. Only intuition, resting on sympathetic understanding of experience, can reach it."

This level of trust in intuition is not unusual for any of the modern-day geniuses we studied either. Most had a very hard time attempting to explain their decisions in a literal sense. They just knew how they felt and what things they saw clearly or not. Their level of intuition and willingness to trust their gut is extreme.

Painter Pablo Picasso once told a friend, "I don't know in advance what I am going to put on the canvas any more than I decide before-hand what colors I am going to use. Each time I undertake to paint a picture, I have a sensation of leaping into space. I never know whether I shall land on my feet." What Picasso is saying here is that he followed his intuition (genius) wherever it led him. He is not trying to control it, he is just trusting his gut and going with the flow.

Poet Robert Frost spoke about his process for writing poetry as one of "carrying out some intention more felt than thought." Author Isabel Allende says of her books, "In a very organic way, books don't happen in my mind, they happen somewhere in my belly. I don't know what I am going to write about because it has not yet made the trip from belly to the mind."

Learning to trust your intuition will be one of the more significant exercises you will do on your way to your 5th Level of performance.

Genius Thoughts

Here are some thoughts on trusting your intuition from some of the geniuses interviewed for this book.

Randy Haykin on
Learning Your Talents

"Early on I was pushed to be very self-aware and true to myself. My parents used to give me batteries of tests in high school that helped me understand my natural talents better. My whole life I think I have been taught to follow these talents and not focus on acquiring tons of others. I carried those lessons with me to college where at Brown I took sixteen classes that had nothing to do with each other, all in an attempt to find out which ones resonated with my natural talents the best. At Harvard I took all sorts of classes on exploring self-awareness.

"One of my talents is for putting people together and creating relationships. People call me the "gardener" because I'm always cultivating productive relationships among others. An example of this is a club I created we call the *Boys of Breakfast*. For the last six years, a group of us here in town have gotten together for breakfast once a month to explore what life is about, discuss each other's challenges and accomplishments, and dive into what makes each of them who they are and help find their direction to their own happiness or success. I always trust my gut when it comes to making decisions in this area. I try very hard not to rationalize around that inner voice telling me what it thinks is the right direction to take."

Anthony Robbins on
Discovering Talents

"I have always believed that one of my talents has been for loving people and having passion for making a difference in their lives. Understanding others and communicating with them and being very good at being able to sense their emotions, fears, desires and needs is perhaps one of my best talents, but I've built my entire life around another talent which I didn't learn I had until the 10th Grade.

"Speaking or making an impact on others emotionally wasn't a talent I was aware of until my junior year of high school. One of my teachers, Mr. Cobb, came to me after speech class and looked into my eyes deeply. After this long pause, he said, 'In all my years of teaching speech, I've never seen a student have more compelling power to move and influence people. When you get up you don't do a speech, you don't talk about anything you are not passionate about.' He knew more about me than I think I did at the time and he asked me to compete in this speech competition just one week away. I gave that speech and I won that competition and it changed my life. He showed me, and convinced me, that if I was completely sincere and passionate and told the truth and just let myself be myself, I could really impact the world with my talents.

"Trying to use a strategy or be something you are not may deliver some results; it may work for a while, but being inauthentic long-term, you aren't going to be happy. How do you take your talents and tie it into the role that is most aligned with those talents and maximize them, that ability is the real difference! I even recently told one of my sons, who was trying to duplicate what I do, 'You have all the words, you have the concept, you put the hard work in, you have the drive, but you are trying to be me—but you are not me. You are something more powerful than me—you are you. You doing you will be more powerful than you trying to do me.'"

Mickey Rogers on
Trusting Your Talents

"Intuition comes into play when you are designing the shot (i.e. the demolition explosion). You have to be able to see clearly in your head how to set the charges to take the building down just where your client needs it to go. There are a lot of books on the technique of how to demolish structures, but when it comes right down to it you touch it, you feel it. There's just a feeling that almost overwhelms me that says, 'I don't care what the books say, this needs to go this way instead.' That's when my gut is talking to me big time, and I just have to listen to it. I don't have a choice.

"Each shot is completely different, and each time my gut is what guides me to the greatest extent. Now I'm not saying that things like experience, knowledge and practiced skill are not important, or that you just suck your thumb, stick it in the wind and take a guess. But I learned early on that my intuition was very good for what needed to be done to make the shots work just right.

"As I walk the shot my gut is talking to me very loudly and I will make changes to the blast sequence, or timing, or anything that just doesn't 'feel right.' Even though the shot has been set according to the way all the books and experts say, if my gut doesn't feel right about how something is, I go with it. That textbook isn't standing there and isn't able to see all the variables I see, but I think my gut is, my intuition, my subconscious mind. It sees all of those aspects that my conscious mind may have missed, and it tries to communicate what it sees to my conscious mind, but it's in such a soft way that most of the time I can't clearly define what it is saying, but I can feel it. So my gut almost always wins out over my head in those moments. Ninety-nine percent of the time my gut gets the final vote. I call it rock-sense instead of common sense."

R | Chapter 7 Review

Chapter 1:
- "The Problem" is an epidemic of people that feel unfulfilled, dissatisfied and frustrated with their performance.

Chapter 2:
- To find out why, we created the Genius Project, and what we found were two key things:
  - There is no one "Genius Talent"; and
  - Self-Awareness and Authenticity are present in higher levels in the best performers.

Chapter 3:
- The myth of strengths and weaknesses supports our turning left instead of right.
- Geniuses turn right significantly more than they turn left.

Chapter 4:
- The effects of the problem go beyond performance issues to include negative physical and emotional effects.
- Inauthenticity causes you to feel upside down, always putting in more effort than you feel you get back in results, and blocks you from your passions and being in the flow.

Chapter 5:
- Today's organizations have shifted from an industrial to an intellectual economy.
- Legacy beliefs left over from the old industrial economy cause dependence and inauthenticity that damages individual performance.

Chapter 6:
- The first step in the solution is to prepare to change by deciding that:
  - You are in charge of your own success;
  - You get what you accept; and
  - You refuse to accept mediocrity.

Chapter 7:

- The first revolution is to understand where your talents and non-talents come from (i.e. voices in your head), and how they create masters and blind spots which you see well or miss altogether.
- The more you are *reacting*, instead of *reasoning*, the more your masters take over.

CHAPTER 8

Revolution #2– Choose Thyself

*"One day Alice came to a fork in the road and saw a Cheshire
cat in a tree. 'Which road do I take?' she asked. 'Where do
you want to go?' was his response. 'I don't know', Alice
answered. 'Then,' said the cat, it doesn't matter."*

~ LEWIS CARROLL

When Lewis Carroll wrote these lines in his book, *Alice in Wonderland*, he may not have realized how poignant they were when it comes to becoming a genius—that before you can get somewhere you have to know where that somewhere is.

In Soren Kierkegaard's *Point of View*, he stresses man's ethical imperative to live an authentic life. For Kierkegaard the most important aspect of choosing who you are is to choose with passion, to become infinitely interested in existing, and not to simply know who you are, but to become it.

In order to become the genius that you can, you need to do more than just know yourself (i.e. possess great self-awareness). You must also then live authentically according to that self-knowledge.

Geniuses are two things: self-aware and authentic. Now that you have met your genius and become more self-aware, you have the first part of the puzzle. The next step in the process is to create a vision for where you want to go that is as authentic as possible.

~ You may not be able to control what talents you possess, but you can definitely control what you do with them. ~

Creating a clear picture of where you want to go is vital to reaching the 5th level of performance. Without this guide, it is easy to get lost or hesitate. Just as the racecar driver needs to know the race course in order to maximize performance, so too do you need to be completely aware of where you are going. Your natural talents may be a Ferrari, but your understanding of how to use those talents is like the racecar driver's knowledge of the course.

Regardless of the potential of the racecar, when the driver doesn't know the course well, he goes too slowly around one corner and too fast around others, because he isn't exactly sure where he is supposed to go. He hesitates and slows down as he approaches a hill, because he isn't quite sure what lies on the other side. He holds back from committing because of this lack of certainty.

In other words, you must define a path that is your own best way—based on your own natural talents, passion and potential strengths—not blindly follow someone else's best way. You must find your authentic location in life.

Location, Location, Location

There is an old cliché that says the three most important things in real estate are: location, location and location. This is also true in the world of individual performance and success.

If all of us have talents, why aren't we all equally as successful? Though there are lots of contributing factors as to why one person may be more successful than another, one major reason we see such diversity in performance is due to where we live (and I don't mean our street address).

Everyone may indeed have talents, but unfortunately not everyone does as good a job of positioning themselves in a location (i.e. job or role) to match with his or her talents. Many people occupy locations where their success depends on their non-talents more than on their talents. The geniuses among us do a great job of finding or creating a location for themselves that accentuates their strengths and minimizes their weaknesses.

Expanding on the racecar driver analogy, imagine you were a dune buggy. Your natural strengths would be for racing in the desert, over rough terrain, in horrible conditions that required very high body clearance, an insane amount of suspension, lots of raw power and huge tires that get good traction in the soft sand. These are your talents as a dune buggy.

As a dune buggy, however, would it make any sense at all to enter a NASCAR or Formula One race? Obviously this wouldn't make any sense, because the strengths of the dune buggy would be a great disadvantage for races on pavement.

When it comes to finding the right location for our natural talents—the mental ones—this issue of *location* is just as important. Failing to find the right location for your thinking talents will have the exact same impact as not finding the right location for your physical talents.

How much of a genius would Albert Einstein have been as a marriage counselor? Would Oprah Winfrey make a brilliant administrative assistant? Would the world remember Patton the artist, or Van Gogh the military commander? In the wrong location, all of these geniuses would not likely be considered the best at what they do.

You are the best one to determine your optimal location. You are the only one who can hear those voices in your head and understand your own best way.

Instead of attempting to modify yourself to better fit the location you find yourself in, you should choose a location that best fits you and your natural talents.

Understanding your natural talents better, then understanding which location to assume or role to fill, is the key to reaching the

5th level of performance. Geniuses do a great job of finding roles or picking locations where their talents are optimally aligned with the demands of their environments. In a way, you could say that geniuses are expert real estate agents.

The Quiet Path

> *"The measure of a thing is its reality, its true self; to fulfill its own measure, to be entirely what it is meant to be, this is to obey the law of existence."*
>
> ~ PLATO

With human nature being what it is, and the legacy of dependence being as prevalent as it is, people continue to accept locations for themselves that just aren't a good fit at all. Many times they sell themselves on what they think they should be, or what others tell them to be, or what the job says they need to be. Instead of finding their own paths to their best locations, they follow the wrong path.

This kind of path is what I call a *loud path*. So many messages, so much pressure to go here, do that or be this. I call this the loud path because so many voices are telling you to follow it. Your parents, your friends, your boss, society, teachers, even writers like me—all suggesting, cajoling, pushing you toward a specific path. The massive noise from all of these people can become overwhelming and hard to ignore.

As well intentioned as most of this advice may be, the fact remains that the loud path is made up of other people's voices and opinions and not your own. These voices know less about who you really are and what your real talents are for, and the path they champion is more often a less authentic one for you.

It is the path championed by your inner voices that is the wisest one for you to follow. Those inner voices are most familiar with who you are, and in turn they are the ones that really know best which location you should occupy or which path you should take to reach it. Relative to the cacophony of voices that make up the loud path, your truest path is indeed very quiet; so I call it the *quiet path*.

Ancient Chinese texts refer to the Tao (pronounced "dow"), which literally means "way" or "path." Following your quiet path means trusting the sense you feel—your gut—because your true way (Tao) is there—just very subtle or quiet.

Author Henry David Thoreau sums up the thoughts on listening to your inner voice very well when he says, "We are constantly invited to be who we are. So accept these invitations instead of rejecting them." These invitations to follow your own quiet path are easy to ignore or reject, because they are so subtle when compared to the loud path championed by the rest of the world. But learning to hear your inner voices and to follow your quiet path will make all the difference between reaching your 5th level of performance and not.

While the quiet path can be hard to perceive, my five-year-old son, Joseph, provided me with a great example of something that is just as present in our everyday lives, but also just as easy to miss.

Light rays are always there but often difficult to distinguish. We see the effects of their presence as they bounce off objects in our world, but perceiving the actual rays of light themselves can be very difficult. If you've ever seen rays of light streaming from behind a cloud, or shooting through a window into a dark and dusty room, you get the idea.

One night, after reading his bedtime book and turning out all but the nightlight, I laid down with Joe to settle him in. As he lay there facing the nightlight he said, "I can see the lights shooting off the nightlight Daddy." When I looked past him at the nightlight, I didn't see it at first, but then when I squinted my eyes a little—sure enough, single beams of light were shooting out of the nightlight right toward us. It was as if they were shiny, three-dimensional sticks reaching out to us from the center of the light.

While this simple phenomenon of refracted light was exceptionally entertaining to Joe, I couldn't help but consider how symbolic it was that right there in front of me was something ever-present, yet so easy to miss. Seeing it wasn't a matter of it being there or not. It was always there. Seeing it was a matter of whether I was attuned to it, with the right focus.

Your quiet path is very much the same as those rays of light. It is your true path. It is your inner voices constantly talking to you, guiding you toward the right direction, the right course of actions for you to take to achieve your objectives. It is, however, very easy to miss. If you are not attuned to it, if you don't have the right focus, you can become unaware of it and instead end up following the loud path. You need to be alert and present to be able to detect your own quiet path.

I recommend you give it a try. Buy a nightlight and each night, as you lie down to go to sleep, look at this light and squint your eyes until you can see the individual rays of light streaming out toward you. Then remember that those voices in your head are always talking to you, telling you where your quiet path is. It just might be the cheapest investment you ever make in improving your performance.

Genius Action Step #4 will give you an online journal where you can record your thoughts on how well you followed your quiet path—how authentic you were—on a daily or weekly basis. This exercise will create a trend that you can follow over time to see how true you have been to your own quiet path. It will also map your level of satisfaction, stress and performance, so you can see how your level of authenticity has affected these areas of your life as well.

> **G**   **Genius Action Step 4:** Please log into your WYG Online workbook and complete the Authenticity Self-Check.

The Rarity of Success

> *"The person who does too much accomplishes very little. Less is more. The most effective people in business (and life) have the discipline to focus on doing just a few things spectacularly well."*
>
> ~ ROBIN SHARMA

It was Dr. Hartman himself, in a discussion with one of his students on the infinite potential of the individual, who said, "What's a genius? Why, you're a genius. For a genius is nothing but a person who can put all his power into one thought." What Dr. Hartman was saying was that anyone could be a genius. He is referring to the potential performance that can be achieved or unlocked when you understand how to apply yourself and place all of your power (talents) into one thought or task. The trick is in specializing in an area that is authentic to your set of talents.

When it comes to being the very best at something, rarity and exclusivity play a significant role. Basically, the more specialized you become, the more your chances of success increase.

Specialization isn't a new idea. Over two thousand five hundred years ago, Confucius saw the folly in trying to be too many things, when he said, "The person who chases two rabbits catches neither."

The concept is no less true today either. We've all heard the old mantra, "You can't be all things to all people." Well my work has proven to me that this is no less true in reaching your highest level of performance. There is a direct but inverse correlation between the levels of performance one achieves and the scope or degree of specialization they have. Lower to middle levels of performance tend to correlate with broader scopes of practice whereas the higher levels of performance correlate with higher degrees of specialization. In other words, the more you try to be, the less you will likely achieve.

The geniuses I've worked with are anything but generalists. They all specialize in a very fine area of expertise. Think about some of the professionals you know for a moment, like doctors, lawyers, scientists or coaches.

In the medical community, we see a clear association between "the best" and the degree of specialization. Medical professionals have created some of the most specialized levels of practice in any industry. The orthopedic community, a specialization in and of itself already, has developed specialists in the hand, sports medicine, spine, upper extremities and lower extremities, even those who specialize in just elbows.

In law, already a specialization, you see a field that has fractured into narrower and narrower levels of specialization with tax lawyers, trial lawyers, defense attorneys, certain kinds of medical malpractice attorneys who focus on only certain kinds of medicine (perhaps to keep up with the hyper-specialization in the medical community).

Look at Albert Einstein or Stephen Hawking, both genius physicists, but in a specialized kind of physics—theoretical physics (as if physicist wasn't already specialized enough).

Anthony Robbins captures the importance of rarity when he talks about success. "One of the reasons I think a lot of people fail to achieve what they truly want is that they never direct their focus; they never decide to master anything in particular. In fact, I think most people fail in life simply because they *major in minor things*," says Robbins. The person who tries to do everything—be everything—usually accomplishes nothing.

Or take Marshall Goldsmith. He is an executive coach who only works with high-level executives, and only ones in large companies, and only ones who are already very successful. Then he only helps them eliminate a select number of counter-productive behaviors to take them to their next level of performance. Talk about specialized!

> *"I don't know what the key to success is, but the key*
> *to failure is trying to please everyone."*
>
> ~ BILL COSBY

The more specialized you get and the more niche a market you create or serve, the greater the likelihood is that you will reach the 5th level of performance. From purely a monetary perspective, in almost every single category of life or business, specialists significantly out-earn generalists at every turn.

The problem with trying to be all things to all people is that it fails to focus all of your talents in one targeted area. Like the light of the sun focused through a magnifying glass, the more diffuse the focus, the less power it has. The more focused that beam of light is, however, the stronger it becomes. If, as a child, you ever used a magnifying glass to set a leaf on fire on a hot summer day, you understand what I'm talking about. Spreading yourself too thinly has the same diffusing effect on your potential. It just doesn't work. Remember, he who is a jack-of-all-trades is a master of none, and 5th level performance requires mastery. Yes, even the Balanced Pattern, which has all three classes of talent as its masters, has its limitations. Because such people have three masters they do not do well in situations that require them to ignore one dimension—such as becoming too emotionally connected as a nurse, or not being able to operate without a well structured plan.

If you are attempting to be a genius at lots of different things, you will surely have a hard time of it. You might become adequate at many things, but not an expert at any of them. Instead of trying to be good at lots of things, pick something that you love and are very good at and figure out how to become even more specialized in that area, and how to make a living at it.

The diagram below illustrates the concept of increasing your performance by decreasing your scope.

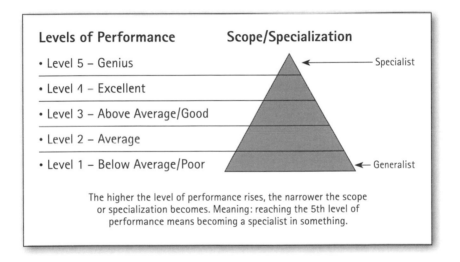

Levels of Performance   Scope/Specialization

- Level 5 – Genius   ← Specialist
- Level 4 – Excellent
- Level 3 – Above Average/Good
- Level 2 – Average
- Level 1 – Below Average/Poor   ← Generalist

The higher the level of performance rises, the narrower the scope or specialization becomes. Meaning: reaching the 5th level of performance means becoming a specialist in something.

Your task in becoming more authentic is to narrow your focus and prune your role to become more exclusive, more rare, more specialized. In so doing, at the same time you prune your dependence on non-talents and leave your success dependent on only that which you naturally do very well.

> "There are a lot of things I stink at. I just make sure
> I don't have to do them to be successful."
> ~ DR. MARSHALL GOLDSMITH

Action Step: To help you determine how you can become more specialized, list your industry below and any sub-categories that exist in that industry. If you can't think of any, that's great because here is your chance to create some. If you get stuck, here are some tips. Look at others to see how they have managed to specialize in their own niche:

- Who in your industry is considered an expert?
- Who do you know that specializes in anything?
- What is one area of your industry that is very complicated or in high demand?
- If you can't think of anything within your industry, could you become a consultant to that industry, thus creating a specialization in the consulting industry?

My Industry: _____

Industry Sub-Categories (areas within that industry that could be considered a specialty):

_____

_____

_____

Based on what you have learned from your Genius Profile, which of the sub-categories above could you specialize in? Which parts of your industry do you find more enjoyable, exciting, interesting and in which parts have you found that you are just plain "better"?

_____

_____

_____

In the next chapter, I will give you an exercise that will involve using these areas as one of your targets for setting goals.

MacGyver Wasn't Real

As you try to find your quiet path, or flesh out your special niche, you cannot force yourself into being something you are not. The location you choose and the specialty role you fill *must* be authentic.

In the mid-1980s, there was a television series in the United States called *MacGyver*. In the show, actor Richard Dean Andersen played secret agent Angus MacGyver, who favored brains over brawn when it came to fighting bad guys. He never used a gun, but in order to accomplish his missions, he would make use of everyday items to craft explosives or a radio or any countless number of cool things. Every episode found MacGyver using little more than his Swiss Army knife and some duct tape to jury-rig some complex device to defeat the enemy. Basically, MacGyver was a genius at jury-rigging solutions for success.

Unfortunately, though, MacGyver wasn't real. You can't jury-rig your success by trying to adapt yourself to something you weren't meant to be. Or at least you can't expect to reach the 5th level of performance if you do. While a kitchen knife might have made a great terminal switch for one of MacGyver's bombs, you can't effectively jury-rig yourself to fit some role that isn't true to who you are and expect to find the levels of satisfaction and success we've been discussing in this book. Yet this is what we see people doing all the time when it comes to improving performance.

In real life, you might jury-rig lots of unimportant things, but when it comes to the truly important aspects of your life, you would never jury-rig them. You would never even consider using a safety pin to hold your child's seatbelt together, for example, or duct tape to hold your car brakes in place. So why would you consider jury-rigging your success by adapting yourself to some role that you weren't meant for, a role that isn't authentic for you?

As you create your new roles in the upcoming step, make sure you don't adapt yourself like one of MacGyver's utensils. Stay true to what you do well, and insist on a role that doesn't require you to jury-rig yourself.

Self-Belief

Before you can achieve your 5th level of performance, you also have to believe in yourself, and to have self-belief requires that you are satisfied with yourself. As Thoreau said, "The man who is dissatisfied with himself, what can he do?"

A significant part of self-belief is *self-acceptance*. As humans, we will all surely fail many times. We will likely fail more than we succeed in many ways. To learn new things requires us to fail more often than we succeed. To reach genius levels of performance also requires us to be very aware of our non-talents and all the things that we are not good at.

Many people dislike their mistakes, though, and view their non-talents as a weakness, a failure, or some kind of shortcoming. This distain for their weaknesses is one of the major driving factors behind their efforts to *fix* those non-talents. In order to truly appreciate yourself, however, you have to *truly* appreciate all that you are—including all that you are not.

There is an old Chinese saying that goes, "Recognize beauty, and ugliness is born. Recognize good, and evil is born." It is impossible to qualify something as good without accepting the existence of things that are not good. You can't learn to love yourself fully, and truly believe in yourself, until you are willing to accept all of your flaws and non-talents as well. You can't appreciate yourself fully without acknowledging all that is you—both good and bad.

The Chinese concept of yin-yang depicts this dichotomy very well. The following image represents the duality that exists in all of nature, in all things and even in you. It represents the light and the dark, the positive and the negative, the right and the wrong—or, for our purposes here, your talents and non-talents. It represents the balance between all things.

The enlightening aspect of this concept is that just as the circle itself is not whole without both the light and dark sides, your acceptance of yourself is not complete without acknowledging both the positives and negatives of who you are—and are not. You cannot feel whole about yourself until you acknowledge both, and without being whole you will never have true self-belief.

Just as understanding your talents is a part of self-awareness, so too is understanding your non-talents. Geniuses understand their non-talents. They shine big, bright lights on their inabilities and readily acknowledge them. Instead of wishing they weren't so, they understand that they must exist in order to allow their other abilities to exist.

To achieve your 5th level of performance, you must give up any misconceptions you have about being good at everything. You are what you are: missing talents and all. And there is nothing unusual about that as the same is true of every other person on the planet.

The geniuses we studied have no more or less raw talent than anyone else. The big difference is that they don't try to hide from this fact, and they don't try to change it either. Instead of wishing they had other talents, they all have high levels of belief that the talents they do have are sufficient to make them a genius in something.

The question you needn't ask yourself is, "How do I get different talents to make me better for my role?" The question 5th level performance requires an answer to is, "What needs to be different about my role to make it better for my talents?"

Future Visioning

We've talked about what location you will occupy in your new authentic future. We've discussed how to find your own quiet path to that location, and you've given thought to why you should believe you deserve to get there. Now let's put all those pieces together into a single cohesive image of your future self.

In the 1960s, Dr. Maxwell Maltz, a plastic surgeon by training, conducted research into how people's images of themselves influenced their perceptions of reality. What Dr. Maltz found was that our minds can't tell the difference between a synthetic experience and a real-world experience—as long as that synthetic experience was sufficiently detailed or real enough. By synthetic experience, I mean *imaginary,* one held strictly in our heads.

If a person creates an image in his or her head that is real enough, even if it isn't real or has never actually existed, he or she is likely to believe it as though it were a reality. This belief can actually affect physical performance as well.

Dr. Maltz wrote a book called *Psycho-Cybernetics,* which details the results of his investigations. In it, he describes the human brain and nervous system as a perfect goal-striving servo-mechanism. "Experimental and clinical psychologists have proven that the human nervous system cannot tell the difference between an *actual* experience and an experience imagined vividly enough and in detail," explains Dr. Maltz.

In the book, Dr. Maltz provides an account of an experiment on the effects of mental practice on improving basketball free throws. The study, published in *Research Quarterly,* divided the subjects into three groups. Each group was tested for free throw accuracy at the beginning and the end of the experiment. The three groups were:

- Group one practiced free throws physically for 20 days;
- Group two performed no practice at all; and
- Group three spent 20 minutes a day getting into a deeply relaxed state and visualizing themselves shooting free throws. When they missed, they would visualize themselves correcting their aim accordingly.

The results were quite remarkable. The first group improved in scoring by 24%. The second group showed no improvement at all, and the third group, which practiced only in their minds, improved in scoring 23%. Amazingly, pure mental practice yielded results almost identical to those seen in the group that practiced physically.

In the book, *Peak Performance, Mental Training Techniques of the World's Greatest Athletes*, Charles Garfield talks about a similar experiment conducted by Soviet sports scientists. The study examined the effect of mental training, including visualization as described by Maltz, on four groups of world-class athletes prior to competing in the 1980 Lake Placid Olympics. Like Maltz, the Soviet researchers also found that pure mental training created actual improvements in physical reality.

The findings of research like this show that if you believe in something firmly enough, and can create an image of it in your head that is clear enough, your mind will accept it as real.

The opposite is also true, in that if you don't possess a clear enough image for some aspect of your life, your mind will not believe in it, and your attitude toward it will be like that of any other thing you don't really believe in (i.e. speculative, unconvinced, uncertain, etc.).

The same is true for being authentic and choosing your direction in life. To help focus your drive, motivation and all of your natural talents, you need to have a crystal-clear vision for where you are going. You need to create a vision for yourself that is so real that you cannot only see it, but you can actually feel it, smell it, taste it and almost remember it as if it has already happened. I have a friend in Glasgow, Scotland who can give us a good example of this level of clarity.

One day, while I was having lunch with Gerry and another friend named Allan, Gerry started describing his plans for what he was going to do once his business took off. He envisioned himself buying a ranch in Jackson Hole, Wyoming in the United States. As he started to describe the house he would build, he went into such detail that even Allan and I could see it. At one point he described the master bedroom, and the picture window it would have overlooking the property, and the skylight above and how the sun would shine in at certain times of the day. No detail was left out, and by the time he had finished describing this one room, I swear I could actually feel the warmth of the mid-day sun shining down on my face.

This is the level of clarity you must have for your direction in life, your point B on your life map if you will. And one way I've found to help people do this is an exercise I call *Future Visioning*. The goal is to develop a vision of yourself in the future that is so clear and real that your mind can't tell the difference. As a result, your mind commits itself and its resources to this vision just as if it were real.

When this happens your certainty goes way up, your conviction increases and you start to see any indecisiveness you had go away. You truly will believe that this future vision is as much a reality as anything you can remember from the past.

When it comes to creating this future vision, the past can actually help. Outside of the fact that your past actually happened and *was* real, the reason it seems real to you is because of the level of detail. When you remember a past event, there are millions of little pieces to that memory that you probably didn't even notice (e.g. the shadowing of a light on a table, the small cracks on the wall, the dust in the corner, the countless objects in the room that you never consciously acknowledged). The level of detail for things remembered is what makes that memory so real, and it is your subconscious mind that provides most of this sense of reality, as it is the one capable of recognizing so much detail. Think of the difference in detail between a photograph and a painting.

The problem is that many people fail to create a vision for where they are going that is sufficiently detailed or real enough to actually win their minds over and enlist all of their strengths and talents. They create fuzzy goals or an incomplete vision. The result is that they achieve fuzzy or incomplete results.

To create a vision of your future that will be real enough to focus your talents, release your doubts, gain your commitment and drive you towards achieving it, you must create a similar level of detail—a level approaching that of a past, remembered event or time.

The Future Visioning exercise is simply a process of using your past to help ensure a similar level of detail for where you see yourself in the future. To do this, please go to your WYG online workbook, where you will find the Future Visioning exercise. Remember to make it as focused and specialized as possible.

Once you have completed your Future Visioning exercise, print it out and refer to it regularly. Make changes to it as things change in your life. I recommend making it part of a quarterly life review, just like any good business person reviews his or her goals and objectives on a regular basis.

And remember, no level of detail is too small for this exercise. Just like the picture, the higher the resolution, the greater the level of detail, and the greater the detail, the more your subconscious mind will believe in and chase your vision.

> *Note: This exercise may take you several hours, even days, to complete, as you will want to give it careful consideration. This is your future you are creating, so take your time and trust that the effort you put in will return much greater results.*

In the end, this entire Choosing Thyself chapter can be distilled into one very simple message: "To become a genius, figure out what you enjoy most, and find a way to do more of it—a whole lot more."

Genius Thoughts

Here are some thoughts on the Rarity of Success from one of the geniuses I interviewed for this book.

Dan Lyons on Specializing Your Talents

"I was hyper-competitive so much of my early life that I had to become very aware not only of what I was very good at, but also what I did not do well. In this process, I learned that when I tried to do things that relied on my non-talents, I didn't perform well. This meant that I let others down, and I didn't win. The result was that I learned early on to excise those things that I didn't do well, because they depended on my being excellent at things I wasn't excellent at. Since I wanted so desperately to win, I realized that to make sure I won all the time, I had to play to my strengths and only compete in areas where my talents could be capitalized. So you could say that my discovery of becoming authentic to my natural talents and non-talents was driven by my desire to please others and win. From then on I learned to focus only on being true to my natural talents, which fed my ability to succeed and win.

"I know we're talking about my mental talents, but my physical talents make a great analogy. When I was young, my dad said to me, 'There's no reason you can't run a ten-second 100-meter race.' Now there are lots of reasons why I can't run a ten-second 100-meter race, but my build and musculature made me a very good cross-country runner. Trying to compete at everything like I did back then, it took me a while, but eventually I realized that my natural physical talents were such that they made me a very good long-distance runner. But those same elements made me not a great 100-meter sprinter. That same understanding for the physical world carried over to the mental world, and I eventually learned that the same principle holds true: the natural mental talents I have make me very good at some things and not good at others. The message is the same on either side of the analogy: become great at what your talents will make you great in, and let the rest go. You can't do it all."

R | Chapter 8 Review

Chapter 1:
- "The Problem" is an epidemic of people that feel unfulfilled, dissatisfied and frustrated with their performance.

Chapter 2:
- To find out why, we created the Genius Project, and what we found were two key things:
  - There is no one "Genius Talent"; and
  - Self-Awareness and Authenticity are present in higher levels in the best performers.

Chapter 3:
- The myth of strengths and weaknesses supports our turning left instead of right.
- Geniuses turn right significantly more than they turn left.

Chapter 4:
- The effects of the problem go beyond performance issues to include negative physical and emotional effects.
- Inauthenticity causes you to feel upside down, always putting in more effort than you feel you get back in results, and blocks you from your passions and being in the flow.

Chapter 5:
- Today's organizations have shifted from an industrial to an intellectual economy.
- Legacy beliefs left over from the old industrial economy cause dependence and inauthenticity that damages individual performance.

Chapter 6:
- The first step in the solution is to prepare to change by deciding that:
  - You are in charge of your own success;
  - You get what you accept; and
  - You refuse to accept mediocrity.

Chapter 7:
- The first revolution is to understand where your talents and non-talents come from (i.e. voices in your head), and how they create masters and blind spots which you see well or miss altogether.
- The more you are *reacting*, instead of *reasoning*, the more your masters take over.

Chapter 8:
- Choose a place where you want to go that is authentic.
- Make it authentic and real (not forced or jury-rigged).
- Believe that you can.

CHAPTER 9

Revolution #3— Create Thyself

"Create the self you will be happy to live with all your life. Make the most of yourself by fanning the tiny spark of possibility into flames of achievement."

~ FOSTER MCCLELLAN

Congratulations, you are almost done! In truth, you're only getting started, because being authentic is a never-ending process of being ever vigilant and adapting to new duties, new goals and a new direction in which life constantly takes you—while staying true to who you are. For now, though, you have evolved from being blind to any inauthenticity in your life and subject to a legacy of dependence to realizing that you must be authentic—that you must become your own SEO. You have gained a greater understanding for your true genius, and you have created an image of the authentic self you want to become.

Here's a riddle for you. If there are three frogs sitting on a log, and one decides to jump into the water, how many frogs are left on the log? The answer is three, because deciding to jump and actually jumping are two very different things. So far you have been working in your mind. You have been considering your attitude, examining long-held beliefs and gaining new knowledge. And hopefully by now you have decided to jump. Your final revolution, however, is to leave the world of your mind and move into your reality—to actually make the changes in your life that you now know are needed and believe possible. To achieve this final revolution, you must actually turn right to *create* an authentic role for yourself. You must jump!

Comfort Zones

> *"You have to leave the city of your comfort and go into the wilderness of your intuition. What you'll discover will be wonderful. What you'll discover will be yourself."*
>
> ~ *ALAN ALDA*

One of the obstacles that prevents my clients from jumping is that they fail to get out of their comfort zones. Comfort zones include all the things we do frequently simply to feel comfortable. It is much like the *querencia*—a term in bullfighting that refers to the spot in the ring where the bull always returns for comfort. Former CEO of Hewlett-Packard, Carly Fiorina, describes it this way, "Each bull has a different querencia, but as the bullfight continues, and the animal becomes more threatened, it returns more and more often to his spot. As he returns to his querencia, he becomes more predictable. And so, in the end, the matador is able to kill the bull because instead of trying something new, the bull returns to what is familiar—his comfort zone."

> *"Comfort zones are plush-lined coffins."*
>
> ~ *STAN DALE*

It is the comfort zone's job to keep you doing what you've always done. If you try to break out of these old habits and even entertain the idea of doing something different, your comfort zone starts pointing out all the negative reasons why you shouldn't do that, why it is dangerous, why you should be fearful. Your comfort zone will employ whatever tools it has at its disposal to scare you back into your own private quarencia. In *As Man Thinketh,* author James Allen talks about how effectively your comfort zone manages to keep you in check. "If we dare to step outside the bounds of the comfort zone, these tools are used swiftly and with precision," writes Allen.

The weird thing is that you may have become comfortable with being inauthentic, when being authentic should be more comfortable. You may have spent so much time being inauthentic that it actually feels normal, and over enough time you may have become comfortable with being uncomfortable. To be authentic, this must change! You will have to get uncomfortable before you get really comfortable, and this takes courage.

Courage to Change

> *"Not everything that is faced can be changed, but*
> *nothing can be changed until it is faced."*
>
> ~ JAMES BALDWIN

Management theorist W. Edward Deming once said, "It is not necessary to change. Survival is not mandatory." Change requires courage, because change is scary. The best way to overcome this fear of change is to make the fear of *not* changing even greater.

I tell people, "If you make it easier to fail than to succeed, the only thing you will likely succeed at is failing." By this I mean you have to risk something significant enough to make it scarier to fail than to succeed.

In the eighth through eleventh centuries, Viking sailors were an acquisitive lot. They had expanded their Scandinavian empire to include most of the North Atlantic European coastal areas; reaching south to North Africa, east to Russia and even as far east as Constantinople. When it came to invading new lands, legend has it that the Vikings adopted an interesting but effective means of motivating themselves to succeed. When they would land on a foreign coast to conquer its lands, to ensure that it wasn't easier to fail in battle and return to the safety of their boats and the sea, the Vikings would burn their boats. This meant that failure wasn't much of an option, because there was no real ability to retreat. Talk about not having an exit strategy!

While I don't recommend to my clients that they risk their lives as motivation to succeed, I think we can take inspiration from this legend by creating significant consequences to *not* changing, or *not* getting out of our comfort zones. These consequences should be severe enough to help us face our fears of change or persevere in the face of whatever obstacles may stand in our way.

To share my own example of how I have made it harder to fail than to succeed, when I joined the Navy, I signed on to become a search and rescue (SAR) swimmer. As an enlisted person, I signed a contract which meant that for the next six years the U.S. Navy owned me—literally. In return, they would provide me with the opportunity to *attend* all the special schools required to become a SAR swimmer.

This did not, however, guarantee I would pass these schools, just that they would allow me to try. If I failed, the Navy still owned me, and if I couldn't take on the role of rescue swimmer, they would assign me to another role. The big problem with this, though, was that the assignments for those who failed their schooling were usually all the jobs that no one volunteered for in the first place (like chocking chains on a carrier deck, which involves running under a jet or helo, often with engines running, and using chains to chock (tie) her down—which is also one of the most dangerous jobs in the military, by the way).

Knowing that the SAR program had one of the highest attrition rates of all military training programs (approximately 64% of students fail to graduate), I figured failure wasn't an option. My six-year contract was my "boat." If I failed, I was the property of the U.S. Navy for six long years, likely filling a miserable role I would hate.

There were many times—as I lay there unable to feel most of the muscles in my body and wishing I couldn't feel those I could because they hurt like hell—that I contemplated dropping on request. I watched a good many classmates hit their personal wall and give up. As they gave the brass bell three slow rings (the signal that they were voluntarily quitting), I was often tempted to follow suit. In the end, my desire to win, along with the dread of being stuck in a miserable job for six years, was enough to keep me still.

Had I been in a situation where quitting was easier than persevering (e.g. had quitting meant I would have been let out to return home to a safe and average civilian job), then maybe the temptation to quit would have been much greater. As it was, though, the prospect of quitting was much less attractive than staying, and that's the point behind this message. I made sure it wasn't easier to fail than to succeed, so I succeeded.

~ If you make it easier to fail than to succeed, the only thing you will likely succeed at is failing. ~

Some years later, I did the same thing when I started my own consulting company. Having a nice job at Johnson & Johnson meant security, great benefits, a company car and all the advancement one could ask for with over 172 sister companies to move up in. Such security is incredibly important to a young guy with a new family to provide for. But when I walked away from that security to start my own business, it meant I had to succeed.

If you think the attrition rate for SAR school is bad, try starting your own small business. At the time, over 50% of all new businesses failed to survive past the first twelve months, and 95% failed to make it past the five-year mark. When I quit, I walked away from a steady, six-figure income only to invest every last bit of savings, take out a second mortgage on the house and assume significant credit card debt to start the business. If I failed, we would lose everything.

Failing to succeed would definitely be harder than succeeding, and so with that firmly in mind I stepped off to burn my second boat. I quit Johnson & Johnson and put it all on the line. Thankfully, ten years later, the business is still alive and growing.

Having a dream is great, and being tired of where you are is important, but what boat will you burn to ensure that you become the authentic genius you deserve to be?

For some it might be a personal boat, like the public embarrassment of telling everyone you are going to change, but then having to admit to them that you failed to do so. For others it might be a financial boat, as in throwing off the golden handcuffs that bind you to your current role to pursue your dream job, or even create your own dream company.

What will you put on the line to ensure that you succeed in becoming the genius that you know you can be?

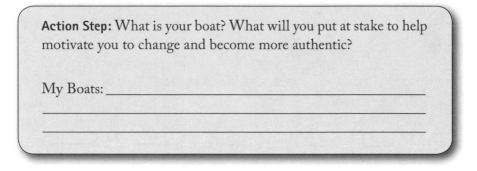

Action Step: What is your boat? What will you put at stake to help motivate you to change and become more authentic?

My Boats: _____

_____

_____

> *"The greatest contributors in life are those who, though afraid at the knock at the door, still answer it."*
>
> ~ DR. STEPHEN COVEY

An Atypical Definition of Success

While it didn't show up anywhere in the hard data, there is one trait which showed up time and time again in the interviews I conducted. One of the questions I asked each interviewee was, "How do you define success?" In almost every single case, every person gave me a very different answer from the one that I expected.

I was expecting to hear that they defined success as the achievement of business goals, or the money they had made, or fame, or power, or some other more typical definition of success. What I heard, however, was that they defined success as "being happy." When I asked them what they were happy about, I was equally surprised. Again the happiness they described didn't have anything to do with fame, power, money or what one might expect. What they were happy with was the relationships they had with their families and friends, or the feeling they got from helping others, or the satisfaction they received from their ability to give back, or the passion they felt for what they did.

Were they happy because they were successful, or was their happiness a key component to their success? In the end I've decided it was the latter, and that their happiness was a key driver of their success, not the result of it. I say this because, from a purely logical perspective, I can think of lots of people who have loads of money, tons of fame, piles of achievements and tremendous power and authority—but who are still not happy. However, all the people I know who consider themselves truly happy also consider themselves truly successful. Therefore, happiness must be the key ingredient in defining your success, not the result of it. It seems that happiness is the DNA of success.

All roads branch out from this, and all lead back to it. Just think about it. You desire success so that you can have lots of money so that you can be financially secure—which will make you happy (you hope). You want to win the competition because you feel the need to prove yourself and have others admire you, which will make you feel better about yourself—which will make you happy (again, you hope). You have a desire to be in charge, on top, the big boss, to have control and prestige, to prove your worth—which will make you really happy.

The key is, everything is really driven by happiness, and so success at its most basic level is built on being happy, not on being *successful* in and of itself. The trick is figuring out what will really make you happy because when you know this, only then do you really know what success means to you.

~ *Happiness is the DNA of success.* ~

Many of us, however, get caught up in chasing a means to an end, spending a life pursuing the trappings of *success*, not the happiness that makes up its true spirit. We get easily confused about what the true objective is and many times end up sacrificing our happiness in pursuit of some objective that was supposed to deliver our happiness in the first place. In such cases, the means actually become the end itself, and the end of our happiness as well.

One person might get so focused on winning manager of the year that she ends up hurting others, even those she loves—which ultimately makes her unhappy. Another person might get so wrapped up in rising high in the organization that the ballast he jettisons to achieve such altitude ends up being his personal life—which ultimately makes him unhappy. Still another person might get lost in the race to acquire so much wealth and security that by the time he has it, he has alienated all those he would share it with—and he is unhappy.

I knew a guy once whom most would view as extremely successful, at least by the more traditional definition of the word. He had all the conventional trappings of success. He had started his own business, and as CEO he had the power and control most assume is tied to success. His company went international and was a financial success, so he had all the money he could ever need. He had somewhat of a public fame, and thousands followed his advice and bought his profiles, which qualified him as successful.

But was this man really successful? From the outside absolutely, but from the inside, he wasn't at all. To achieve his businesses success, he had sacrificed *true* success—happiness. I've never known an unhappier "successful" person in my life. Sure, he put on a good front in public, but when you got behind the curtain he was angry, volatile, hostile, explosive, insecure and fearful that all he had built would somehow be taken away.

He had sacrificed his relationships with his children and wives. He had sacrificed his health. He had sacrificed his closest friendships, and eventually he came to run his company primarily through intimidation and fear. In the end, he had fallen into the trap of chasing the means, not the end. To the world, he was a shining example of success. To himself, however, he was a miserable wreck of a man who felt hollow and unhappy deep inside (as he admitted one time during a private discussion late one night).

Many (all too many, unfortunately) fight so hard to get the trappings of success that they damage or destroy that which would really make them happy. The vital lesson that we should all take from the geniuses around us is not to get caught up in the means to the end.

To be successful means to be happy. So figure out what will *really* make you happy, then chase *that* end—always.

> **Action Step:** To help you define what success means to you, what is your definition of happiness?
>
> My happiness is: _____
>
> _____
>
> _____

Genius Math 101 (Unleashing Your Genius)

"Deep within man dwell those slumbering powers, powers that would astonish him, that he never dreamed of possessing; forces that would revolutionize his life if aroused and put into action."

~ Orison Swett Marden

So, unlike the three frogs, how do you go past *deciding* to jump to actually taking the leap? How do you take the work you've done so far in this book—all of which has involved *deciding* to jump—and actually squeeze the trigger? It's a surprisingly simple process actually. It's simple because you have already done the bulk of the work. It's simple, because when you create better alignment between your role and your talents, performance will increase almost by itself. You don't have to work as hard to be better when you rely on what your brain already does well.

Basically, squeezing that trigger involves a very straightforward process of decreasing dependence on non-talents and increasing dependence on talents. I call it "maximizing your dependence on strengths and minimizing your dependence on weaknesses." There is a sort of math to doing this, which I call *Genius Math*.

The formula below captures the basics of Genius Math. It's a matter of:

- Adding responsibilities to your role that depend on your talents; and
- Subtracting responsibilities in your role that depend on your non-talents.

The responsibilities you add will be those that *are not* currently part of your role but will increase your dependence on your natural talents. The responsibilities you subtract will be those that currently *are* part of your role but that rely on your non-talents.

That's it! Using your Genius Profile, identify one talent that you can increase your dependence on and identify one non-talent that you can decrease your dependence on. It's really as simple as addition and subtraction (i.e. add strength-based responsibilities and subtract weakness-based responsibilities).

You will do this one set at a time (one talent and one non-talent) and then just repeat the whole process until you are happy and satisfied with your performance.

$$((+T) (-NT)) \infty$$
- **Add one Talent**
- **Subtract one Non-Talent**
- **Repeat**

Many times, management assigns responsibilities to a job arbitrarily out of convenience or even just as a random assignment (e.g. someone's got to do it). A great many role expectations are created without much thought, if any, for the natural talents of the person. Many times, roles are created that are looking for a superhuman set of abilities that are just down right impossible to find in one person.

I've seen thousands of roles that were looking for someone who was: empathetic yet detached, detail-oriented yet big-picture focused, competitive yet cooperative, compassionate yet aggressive, or strategic yet tactical. It's ludicrous to think that anyone could be all this, at least to a degree approaching 4th or 5th level performance anyway.

The best thing you can do to help yourself reach higher levels of performance is to change the way you fulfill a role based on what works best for you. Often, a great deal of the competencies that managers list are purely subjective and have little to do with reality anyway (trust me, one of the core deliverables at my company is helping corporate clients determine exactly what competencies are really needed in a given job, and many of them don't have a clue). Changing the requirements of a role means working with the same objectives, but finding new ways to reach them. It requires flexibility to adjust how you fill your role.

Role Flexibility

When we start talking about making changes to your role, it's sort of a given that this is aided by your having some flexibility or control over your role (duh, I know). If you work for someone else, or at a level where you have little say in what your duties are, you will need to achieve some level of role flexibility before you can work on becoming authentic.

Role flexibility is the level of ability you have for changing your role, what responsibilities you have, the tasks and duties that you are expected to perform. Entrepreneurs have high levels of role flexibility, and the higher you go in management the more flexible your role typically becomes as well. But even if you don't have that much flexibility in your role, there are still things you can do to make your role more authentic.

If you don't have enough role flexibility, one of the best ways to convince your manager or organization that giving you some flexibility would be in their best interests is to share this book with them. Maybe 197,000 people can convince them if you can't. It's imperative that you get some flexibility in your role, because if you can't remove responsibilities that rely on your non-talents, it's unlikely that you will reach your 5th level.

Of course, as Michael Lorelli said earlier in this book, sometimes it really is easier to ask for forgiveness than permission. Therefore, if you need to move some things around, lean on someone else or swap tasks, then maybe you should just do it anyway! If you ask and are refused permission to modify your role, consider how you could modify your role without permission—without breaking any rules or getting fired of course.

Why am I suggesting you do something without permission? Because you are your own SEO. You are the one responsible for your success—no one else. Of course, if you have flexibility, use it, but if something in your role depends on one of your non-talents, and you can't get permission to offload that responsibility somehow, then you might want to ask yourself if it is better to offload it without permission and improve your performance than to continue to depend on it and give up performance.

Remember, geniuses refuse to settle! All those I interviewed agreed that sometimes you just have to leave a role if it is too inauthentic. Like Michael Lorelli also says, "If your role is just too inauthentic, you either have to suffer through, or change roles, because you can't change your DNA."

Three Steps to Authenticity

> *"Fish Gotta Swim—Birds Gotta Fly."*
> ~ Oscar Hammerstein—J. Kern

There are three core ways to adjust your role to become more authentic, and these are where you are going to make your jump. Those three options are:

- Talent Bartering—partnering to improve dual role performance;

- Dump & Grab—change the way you perform your own role; and
- Change Roles—change roles altogether.

Option #1—Talent Bartering: This means finding someone who has a talent where you do not, partnering with someone who is strong where you are weak, and vice versa. This is where you partner with someone else to swap or barter each other's complimentary talents. This may happen officially with permission, but many times it is unofficial as well. This is often the case with high-level executives who create collaborative relationships with someone else who can carry out the duties that the other should not, because it would rely on their non-talents (forcing them to manufacture a weakness).

Many leadership development programs tell you that in order to be a great leader, you have to smooth the edges and fill in any holes. They say, "To become a better leader you need to become more *well rounded.*" The higher up the ladder you go, the more likely you are to hear this kind of advice. When you are the top executive, you are expected to be better at most things than those you lead. We hear this so often, but it just isn't true. How many top executives do you know who are excellent at certain things, but just down right horrible at others?

For example, many times we find sales managers who are very good sales managers, but they were not the best sales people. How many great sports coaches do you know who were the *star* athlete? Sure, the great sales managers and the great sports coaches both played the game, and maybe they even performed very well, but in most cases they weren't the star. Just because you lead sales people doesn't mean you have to be a better salesperson than they are. Your job isn't to sell—it's to lead. You aren't supposed to be a better sales person, just a better leader. This is because the talents it takes to lead a team of athletes or sales people are very different than those it takes to be the individual star player or sales person.

"No man has the ability to step outside the shadow of his own character."
~ MAXIMILIEN ROBESPIERRE

When you find yourself responsible for something that relies on one of your non-talents, outsource it. And many times this means swapping duties with someone else who is also struggling with his or her own issues of dependence on a non-talent. Collaborate with someone who has a talent that compliments your non-talent, and vice versa. One example of such a swap can be seen with Kae and Kristy.

Kae was an administrative assistant in the newsroom at a local NBC affiliate. One of her duties was to compile and analyze certain reports. While Kae had a tremendous master for the Heart dimension, she had a big blind spot for the Head dimension. She was not naturally talented when it came to conducting such analysis. No more did she like it than she was good at it, but it was an assigned responsibility she could do nothing about, so she turned left and tried to *fix* her ability to compile and analyze data.

Working in the same newsroom was an associate producer named Kristy who served as the assignment desk editor. Kristy was suffering from her own dependence on a non-talent. She was responsible for taking calls from the public with ideas for news stories and newsworthy events happening in the community. Kristy's blind spot for the Heart dimension made this work not only not enjoyable, but she wasn't very good at it either.

Once Kae and Kristy figured out that each of them had a talent that the other could benefit from, they worked out a talent barter. Kae would take the calls for Kristy and organize them by degree of interest, and Kristy would build the reports for Kae and run the analysis on them. While ideally management would have approved such a swap, when Kae and Kristy asked management their request to swap duties was denied. As their own SEOs, however, they took it upon themselves to do it anyway. The results were two happier and more productive people who stayed with the company a long time.

Action Step: What are two aspects of your current role that force you to rely on a non-talent (based on your "non-talents list" in your Genius Profile—Pg. 6)?

1. _____

2. _____

Name some people you know, at work, who excel in these areas.

_____

_____

What are two aspects of your current role that *do* allow you to rely on a talent (based on your "talents list" in your Genius Profile—Pg. 5)?

1. _____

2. _____

Can you think of anyone at work who isn't good in these areas and whom you could collaborate with to help them fill their own blind spots?

_____

_____

Think of how you could partner with someone to end your reliance on non-talents and help them do the same by helping them handle some of the things that rely on their non-talents. Talk with this person, or persons, about creating some talent bartering collaborations. *If you don't know who has talents in areas where you do not, have them take the Genius Profile. It is free after all.*

Option #2—Dump & Grab: If there isn't anyone with whom you can barter or swap duties, then you may have to *dump* certain responsibilities, and sometimes you may have to *grab* other responsibilities that rely on your talents.

Let's discuss dumping things first. If you have a dependence on a non-talent, but there isn't anyone to collaborate with, talent bartering isn't an option. In these cases you will just have to dump the responsibility from your plate. The most well-known form of this kind of role adjustment is called delegating. Delegating is not bartering, mind you. When you delegate, you aren't trading duties like you would in talent bartering.

The geniuses I spoke to delegate all the time. Anthony Robbins leaves the negotiation of contracts and acquisitions to others who don't share his level of empathy and are more comfortable carrying out *tough* negotiations. Marshall Goldsmith has a University named after him and owns a consulting firm, but he leaves the direct management of both to others because he doesn't enjoy or feel he is good at directly managing others in those kinds of environments. Michael Lorelli delegates all the time, too. In our discussion on how he deals with non-talents, he said, "If it's simply not in my DNA, I try to align myself better, not change myself. I supplement my non-talents through others and delegation instead."

One example of delegation can be found in Mark, a district sales manager for a company that sells anesthesia machines to hospitals. Part of Mark's duties involved making sure his sales representatives were well trained in the technical aspects of new products. These products were very technical, and Mark was anything but a "techie." Instead of turning left and trying to develop his ability to *get* the technical side of things, Mark turned right and delegated this responsibility to one of his reps, who was very much a techie. In doing so, he maintained his focus on his genius and put the genius of one of his reps to even better use. Mark benefited, because he wasn't strapped with being directly responsible for something he wasn't any good at, and the sales rep benefited, because not only did he prove his value to management, but his compensation was adjusted to incorporate his extra work in training and supporting other accounts on the technical side. Actually,

Mark helped the sales rep with his own task of grabbing duties that rely on his talents.

Sometimes delegating isn't even necessary. Often, it is possible just to dump a task altogether by completely getting rid of it. You have to ask yourself if it is a vital part of the role, or if it is left over from all those who did the role before you—some inherited part of the role that exists more because it has always existed than for any practical reason. Ask yourself why you would continue to do it. Justify your answer to yourself. "Because they tell me I have to," and "Because that's the way it is done" are miserable answers, so don't accept them from yourself. If you can't find sufficient reason for it to exist, then dump it.

Action Step: Unlike the previous action step, where the tasks or duties were a more integral part of your role, other duties are often just randomly assigned and could just as easily be offloaded or even done away with completely. Think of two tasks or duties of your role that: A) rely on your non-talents, and B) are not truly vital to your achieving your overall objectives or goals.

1. _____

2. _____

Ask yourself if these duties or tasks really make sense. Are they there because they have always been there? Are they really practical? Look at the example we saw in Gretchen, where the responsibility to make a certain minimum call quota each day was limiting her ability to achieve. In the end, the daily call quota wasn't really an important part of the job. It was more than likely something a manager created to try to improve performance. It's doubtful that anyone had ever really questioned the efficacy of such a rule, and all it actually did was hurt performance in Gretchen's case.

Take a look at the two tasks you wrote down above, and figure out how to remove them. Can they be delegated, and if so, to whom? Can they just be done away with altogether—as in they are not a necessary step anymore?

Gretchen from Chapter Four was a great example of someone who worked within the system to change the duties of her role and dropped certain aspects of it altogether (she got rid of her daily call quota).

In the Dump & Grab mentality of becoming more authentic, not only do you dump duties that make your success dependent on a non-talent, but you also grab (add) new duties that will help make your success even more dependent on your talents. Grabbing is simply finding new tasks or duties that you can do that aren't currently a part of your job, and Jacob makes a good case study for what this looks like.

Jacob was a production supervisor at a manufacturing company. His natural talents were strongest in the Hand dimension, and he had lots of ability when it came to seeing the practical side of things and figuring out what needed to be done in a real-world sense to improve efficiency. As the production supervisor for the pre-build section of the manufacturing process, Jacob had the responsibility of overseeing the first stage of building the lawn mowers his company manufactured.

Jacob's natural talent for identifying better ways of putting things together (the natural talent for integrative ability) gave him sound insights into how he could not only improve the flow of processes in his own section, but in those of his neighboring sections as well. Without being asked to, he put his thoughts together on these improvements and took them to the other section supervisors, who thought they had merit. Then Jacob shared his ideas with the VP of operations. It turned out that Jacob's ideas were indeed valid, and his company implemented many of them resulting in a three percent decrease in production time (which meant nearly $450,000 in savings to the company). It wasn't long before Jacob was asked to sit on an operations review committee, where he would continue to contribute to quality and efficiency issues within the company.

Jacob is a great example of someone who saw an area where his talents could benefit his success and turned right to grab it. Sometimes you grab the opportunity, sometimes you volunteer, and sometimes you create a responsibility where one doesn't exist. Regardless of how you do it, the key to grabbing is to add duties, tasks or responsibilities to your role that depend on your talents, thus giving them a vehicle through which they can contribute to your success.

Action Step: What's something you think you could contribute that isn't currently a part of that role? What is a duty that you could volunteer for that would allow your success to become even more dependent on your natural talents? What's something you see in your role that needs doing, and that you think you could do well, but which you haven't been asked to volunteer for? Could you grab that responsibility and make it your own anyway?

Write down a couple of things you know you are good at that you could grab and add to your role:

1. _____

2. _____

Take a look at the two tasks you wrote down above and figure out how to grab them. Who could you approach? Could you just do it? When will you make this grab?

Grab date: _____

Option #3—Change Roles: One of the most common reasons for chronic failure and dissatisfaction in a role is chronic inauthenticity. As I said earlier, the first step in creating your authentic self is acknowledging your inauthenticity. Kierkegaard said it best when he said, "Face the facts of what you are, for that is what changes what you are." Many times, when people face the fact of what they are, they find that their roles are just too inauthentic, too far from their quiet path or too dependent on their non-talents. They find that in order to be truly authentic, they would have to delegate or modify the majority of their roles. If this is the case, then the best thing for you to do is probably just find another role altogether.

If you can't learn to love what you do, then you need to go do what you love. If your role is too inauthentic, if you are forced to be more of what you are not than what you are, then quitting to go find a role that will allow you to do what you love is probably your best solution.

The problem with quitting, though, is that it is scary. We've all heard the same old saying, "Winners never quit!" As scary as it may be, shouldn't living a life where you feel you are always making mistakes, always struggling and always more dissatisfied—be even scarier?

Granted, quitting is difficult. Quitting requires you to acknowledge that you're never going to be number one in the world, at least not at this. So sometimes it's easier to put it off, not admit it, and settle for being mediocre. To quote author Seth Godin, the problem is that "you grew up believing that quitting is a moral failure. Quitting feels like a go-down moment, a moment where you look yourself in the eye and blink. Of course you were trying your best, but you just couldn't do it. It's the whole Vince Lombardi thing. If you were just a better person, you wouldn't quit. In reality, geniuses quit all the time. They know what they are good at and what they are not good at, and they quit focusing on that which they are not good at. They choose instead to pour all that energy into getting even better at what they are already naturally good at doing.

We can take a lesson from the wisdom of Jack Welch, former Chairman of General Electric. His philosophy was that if GE couldn't be number one or two in any category or market, they had to either figure out how to be number one or two, or they had to get out of that category. He knew that when you were number one you controlled your own destiny. What Welch was doing, in effect, was turning the entire company right instead of left. Instead of trying to change the entire company he decided only to compete where the natural talents of the organization could make them one of the best.

So forget the humiliation of failure associated with quitting. Realize that quitting the stuff that you don't do well frees up your resources to obsess over what you can do well. Many will tell you,

"Quitting is for losers," but as Seth Godin goes on to say, "Quit or be exceptional...*average* is for losers!" I strongly recommend you read Seth's book on the subject of quitting, called *The Dip*.

I promise you this: Once you shine that light on your inauthenticity, once you embrace the truth of your own quiet path and once you decide to take back control of your own success and stop accepting what you get (even if this means quitting your job), the relief and excitement you feel will be incredible. The positive emotions associated with such a life-changing decision will far outweigh any trepidation you have for the risks that quitting or changing may create. Can you sense just the smallest amount of excitement deep inside you right now at just the thought of being in a whole different place one year from now? Is there a little voice whispering inside right now saying, "Man, wouldn't it be so great to stop settling and be what I know I should be?" The question you have to ask yourself is, "Why not?" Why should you continue to settle? Why should you continue to accept less than what you deserve? Why should you be just above average in one role when another role out there holds the promise to unleash your real genius? Sure you can come up with lots of rational lies, but in the end, why? Get real. Get authentic. Get satisfied.

~ *Quit trying to do that which is not you—just do you!* ~

If you decide that Option #3 is the best option, and changing the role altogether is what you must do, here are a couple of tips to help ensure that you don't just jump from one inauthentic role to another.

Make an internal move: consider moving to another role with your existing company. This should be the first option you explore, because you won't lose all the good will, pensions, leave, knowledge and networks you have developed. This may be a very quick option to rule out, but it should still be your first. Talk with your manager and share what you have learned about yourself, and your thoughts concerning your fit with your existing role. A good manager will want to keep you as a valuable resource, even if that means in another role or even a different division.

Be the interviewer: when you interview for any role (internally or otherwise), don't forget you are your own SEO. Not only are you being interviewed, but you are the interviewer as well. You are interviewing the company just as much as they are interviewing you. You need to know if you are going to be just as satisfied with the job as the job hopes to be satisfied with you. To do that there are four parts to any good job fit that you need to keep in mind:

- What the job requires;
- What the job provides;
- What the person requires; and
- What the person provides.

The following figures depict these four sides of the optimal job/person fit. The job has its two sides (i.e. what it requires and what it provides), and the person has the same two aspects. When you combine these four, you get four quadrants:

- Quadrant #1 finds neither the job nor the individual satisfied;
- Quadrant #2 sees the job satisfied but not the individual;
- Quadrant #3 sees the individual satisfied but not the job; and
- Quadrant #4 finds both the individual and the job satisfied.

In quadrant #2, we see voluntary turnover go up, because, while the job's needs are met, the person is dissatisfied and often quits. In quadrant #3, we see involuntary turnover go up, because, while the person's needs are met, the job is dissatisfied, and the person is fired. In quadrant #1, it's a dead heat to see whether the person quits before he or she is fired. Quadrant #4 is where you want to be, because this is the only quadrant that produces Genius levels of performance.

The company makes a profession out of understanding what the person requires *for* the role, but historically, individuals haven't done nearly as good a job at understanding what they require *from* the role. More often than not, the lion's share of the focus tends to be on satisfying the job. If you look at a job-person fit like matchmaking with couples, it wouldn't make much sense to ask the woman what she wanted without

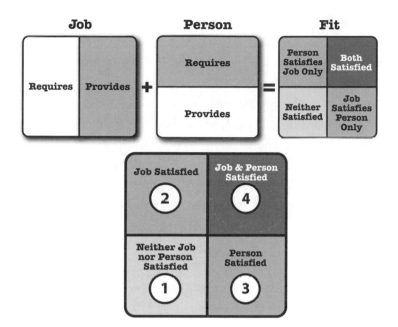

giving equal consideration to what the man wanted, would it? Yet this is what we see far too many times in the world of business.

As your own SEO, you are the one who needs to be responsible for looking after the other side (i.e. what you require compared to what the job provides). By this, I mean specifically:

- How authentic is the job (compared to your talents and non-talents)?
- How well does it align your goals with what you do well naturally?
- Which of your natural talents will the job depend on? and
- Which of your non-talents will it depend on?

You need to take a much closer look at the specific tasks, duties and responsibilities of the job to make sure it will be an authentic fit. Lots of people, even companies, will tell job seekers to "interview the job," but now you have something concrete to go by. Now, in the form of your Genius Profile, you have very specific items to explore to help you gauge the fit of any potential role.

Use the action sheet below to help you gauge how authentic a role will be for you. I realize that sometimes you don't have much of a choice, but if at all possible, resist the tendency to take an inauthentic role. Remember, you get what you accept.

Interviewing the Job: Check Master or Blind Spot next to each dimension according to your Genius Profile, and then consider how important each attribute is in the role you are interviewing. Could you even have the hiring person help you answer this sheet—why not? Simple rule: The less dependence a role has on your blind spots and the more dependence it has on your masters, the better the fit.

M B	Importance in the Job—Dependence				
	Very Low	Low	Some	High	Very High
☐☐ **Head:**					
• Strategic Planning	☐	☐	☐	☐	☐
• Complex Problem Solving	☐	☐	☐	☐	☐
• Creating New Systems & Processes	☐	☐	☐	☐	☐
• Highy Structured	☐	☐	☐	☐	☐
• Intellectual	☐	☐	☐	☐	☐
M B					
☐☐ **Hand:**					
• Action Oriented	☐	☐	☐	☐	☐
• Rapid Response	☐	☐	☐	☐	☐
• Results Oriented	☐	☐	☐	☐	☐
• Urgency	☐	☐	☐	☐	☐
• Practical/Tactical	☐	☐	☐	☐	☐
M B					
☐☐ **Heart:**					
• Emotional Intelligence	☐	☐	☐	☐	☐
• Coordinating others	☐	☐	☐	☐	☐
• Communications	☐	☐	☐	☐	☐
• Leading/Developing Others	☐	☐	☐	☐	☐
• Getting Results Through Others	☐	☐	☐	☐	☐

Squeezing the Trigger

Are you ready? It's time to put the book down, leave the online workbook alone, and take everything you've done to this point and execute!

To start unleashing your genius, I want you to look at pages five and six in your Genius Profile. There you will find the lists of "Talents" and "Non-talents." Pick just one of the talents that you *did not* circle in the action step on page 103 of this book. This is a talent that you are not depending on enough in your current job, and this is going to be the first natural talent you work to maximize your dependence on.

Then pick one of the Non-talents that you *did* circle for the action step on page 104 of this book. This is a non-talent that you are depending on too much, and this is going to be the first non-talent you work to minimize your dependence on. In Genius Math, you always add one and subtract one at the same time.

Select these talents and non-talents based on which ones are most relevant to the roles you fill right now. Go ahead and look at your Genius Profile and the action steps, select these items now and write them down in the space provided below.

My Maximizer (Talent): _____

_____

_____

My Minimizer (Non-talent): _____

_____

_____

Next, decide which of the Talent Bartering or Dump & Grab options would be most appropriate for the items you just selected and give them a try. As I said, it is actually that simple. Granted, you will have your own unique obstacles and circumstances to contend with, and adjusting roles is never easy, but if it were easy to be a genius, everyone would be doing it, wouldn't they?

Use the lessons in this book, specifically chapters seven, eight and nine, as your guide. And remember, the actual process of becoming more authentic doesn't have to be difficult. It just requires that you actually do it.

Add one talent—subtract one non-talent—repeat

It doesn't have to be any more complicated than that. There is no set requirement for level of authenticity either. There is no degree or percentage to focus on. Authenticity is a spectrum and therefore there is no *ideal* level of authenticity. If there is a pure "authentic" and "inauthentic," they exist only at the extreme ends of the spectrum. Most of us exist somewhere in between, but the more we move toward the authentic side (the right side of the Long X), the less we suffer from The Problem, and the more of a genius we become.

I'm not sure who said it, but it was once said, "We're not where we want to be. We're not where we ought to be, but thank God we're not where we used to be." I love this quote, as it's a great acknowledgment of the fact that progress is a journey.

If you decide that talent bartering or adding or subtracting duties won't work, and your role is just too inauthentic, then revisit Option #3 (i.e., change role), and continue on the same journey of progress. Just remember never to settle!

Once you succeed in adding your first talent and subtracting your first non-talent, repeat the whole process. Go back to your Genius Profile, select another set (one talent, one non-talent), and decide how to maximize the talent and minimize the non-talent. Repeat this process, until you can truthfully say you love what you do and are happy and satisfied.

Once you have run through one or two sets of addition and subtraction and reached a point where you are much more authentic, satisfied and performing better, I recommend you complete the post-assessment to reassess how much you have improved. But don't worry if you aren't 100% satisfied just yet. Life is ever-changing, and so you're journey may never end.

You might always be changing this or that to ensure you stay authentic—you probably will. Just make sure you remember what John Lennon said, "Life is what happens to you while you're busy making other plans." Don't forget the discussions on happiness as the DNA of success, and don't substitute this kind of personal development for the other kind and lose sight of the whole purpose of this book—to help you become more satisfied, fulfilled, successful and, in the end, happier.

Authenticity is a journey, not a final destination, so enjoy the ride!

| R | **Chapter 9 Review**

Chapter 1:
- "The Problem" is an epidemic of people that feel unfulfilled, dissatisfied and frustrated with their performance.

Chapter 2:
- To find out why, we created the Genius Project, and what we found were two key things:
    - There is no one "Genius Talent"; and
    - Self-Awareness and Authenticity are present in higher levels in the best performers.

Chapter 3:
- The myth of strengths and weaknesses supports our turning left instead of right.
- Geniuses turn right significantly more than they turn left.

Chapter 4:
- The effects of the problem go beyond performance issues to include negative physical and emotional effects.
- Inauthenticity causes you to feel upside down, always putting in more effort than you feel you get back in results, and blocks you from your passions and being in the flow.

Chapter 5:
- Today's organizations have shifted from an industrial to an intellectual economy.
- Legacy beliefs left over from the old industrial economy cause dependence and inauthenticity that damages individual performance.

Chapter 6:
- The first step in the solution is to prepare to change by deciding that:
    - You are in charge of your own success;
    - You get what you accept; and
    - You refuse to accept mediocrity.

Chapter 7:
- The first revolution is to understand where your talents and non-talents come from (i.e. voices in your head), and how they create masters and blind spots which you see well or miss altogether.
- The more you are *reacting*, instead of *reasoning*, the more your masters take over.

Chapter 8:
- Choose a place where you want to go that is authentic.
- Make it authentic and real (not forced or jury-rigged).
- Believe that you can.

Chapter 9:
- Get out of your comfort zone by finding your courage to risk what it takes to move.
- Define your success by defining your happiness.
- Start unleashing your genius by just doing the math.
- If your role won't flex to your needs, find another role.

Just Do You!

B efore I wrap things up, you might be wondering what ever happened to Lina, whom we met in the opening page of Chapter
One. I worked with Lina to help her identify where she was being
inauthentic. While there were things about her role that she could
change, when she took a good honest look, she decided that her role
was just too inauthentic.

Within a few months, she found a new role with another company
that allowed her to craft her own role from the outset and was much
more authentic overall. Lina is doing great now!

As to the conclusion, when I started my own company, my father
gave me a card with a simple message scribbled on it. It was a rather
famous quote by Henry David Thoreau that read, "Go confidently
in the direction of your dreams! Live the life you've imagined." I still
have this card in my desk, and it continues to inspire me to continue
to drive toward my dreams, not just settle for what I get.

My hope is that in these pages you've taken your own journey and
rediscovered your own genius. I hope that you've developed the self-
respect and courage to admire and respect that Genius. Finally, it is

my sincerest hope that you now know who you are and what unique and great potential you possess, and that you will use this knowledge to go confidently in the direction of your dreams.

Remember:

- Be true to who you are—not who others think you should be;
- Follow your quiet path—don't blindly follow the path of others;
- Do what comes naturally to you; and
- Accept only the best for yourself—never settle.

Basically…**Just Do You!**

About the Author

Jay Niblick is the founder and CEO of Innermetrix Inc. an international consulting firm with offices in five countries specializing in providing full service consulting solutions to professional business consultants and coaches (*www.innermetrix.com*). He is also co-founder and Chief Science Advisor to the online coaching company InnerTalent (*www.innertalent.com*).

As one of the world's leading authorities on the application of Formal Axiology in a business environment, Jay is ideally suited to help you understand your own Genius and how to maximize it.

He holds multiple technology patents, trademarks and copyrights on psychometric instruments and methodologies relating to identifying and maximizing human talent, and is the author of the *Attribute Index* (300,000 copies sold worldwide).

He has been a paid keynote speaker and lecturer around the world in the areas of strategic management, peak performance, executive coaching, leadership development and organizational development.

Jay was among only 14 renowned business thought-leaders and practitioners commissioned to provide essays for *Blueprint For Success*, the landmark reference on individual performance and success.

Jay also sits on the Board of Directors at the Robert S. Hartman Institute (a scholarly project at the University of Tennessee in the United States dedicated to the study of human nature, value and decision-making).

Genius Study Statistics

n=197,000
59% male / 41% female

Geography description:

3% Middle East
4% Asia
7% Australia
12% UK
20% Europe (central and eastern)
54% North America

Industry:

1% Accounting/Auditing
1% Arts, Entertainment, Media
1% Biotech/Pharmaceuticals
1% Community Services, Social
  Services, Non-Profit
1% Education, Training, Library

1% Engineering
1% Information Technology
1% Law Enforcement and
  Security
1% Legal
1% Restaurant/Food Services

Industry (continued):

1% Transportation and Warehousing

2% Computers—Hardware and Software

2% Construction, Mining and Trades

2% Employment Placement Agency

2% Government and Policy

2% Hospitality Services

2% Human Resources

2% Internet/E-Commerce

2% Real Estate

2% Telecommunication

3% Consulting Services

4% Customer Service and Call Center

4% Healthcare Practitioner and Technician

5% Insurance

6% Administration and Support Services

7% Advertising/Marketing/ Public Relations

7% Financial Services

7% Manufacturing

8% Banking

9% Retail/Wholesale

11% Sales

Level:

5% Entry level

17% Senior Executive

18% Mid-Level

27% Management

33% Executive

Genius Study Research (Continued)

Table 1

Item	r =		r =
Accountability for Others	−0.1	Persuading Others	0.1
Attention to Detail	0.2	Practical Thinking	0.5
Attitude Toward Honesty	0.4	Proactive Thinking	0.1
Attitude Toward Others	0	Problem and Situation Analysis	−0.3
Balanced Decision Making	0.3	Problem Management	0.1
Conceptual Thinking	0.4	Problem Solving	0.1
Concrete Organizing	0.4	Project Goal Focus	−0.3
Consistency and Reliability	0	Project Scheduling	0.1
Conveying Role Value	0.2	Quality Orientation	−0.3
Correcting Others	−0.2	Realistic Expectations	0.2
Creativity	0.4	Realistic Goal Setting for Others	0.2
Developing Others	−0.3	Realistic Personal Goal Setting	0.1
Diplomacy	0.3	Relating to Others	0.3
Emotional Control	0.1	Respect for Policies	−0.2
Empathetic Outlook	0.5	Respect for Property	0.4
Enjoyment of the Job	−0.2	Results Orientation	0.1
Evaluating Others	−0.1	Role Awareness	−0.3
Evaluating What is Said	0.4	Role Confidence	−0.1
Flexibility	0.2	Seeing Potential Problems	0.1
Following Directions	0.3	Self Confidence	−0.1
Freedom From Prejudice	0.2	Self Control	0.3
Gaining Commitment	0.2	Self Direction	0.5
Handling Rejection	−0.2	Self Discipline/Sense of Duty	0.2
Handling Stress	0.4	Self Esteem	−0.4
Human Awareness	0.3	Self Improvement	0.1
Initiative	−0.4	Self Management	0.4
Integrative Ability	0.4	Self Starting Ability	−0.2
Intuitive Decision Making	0	Sense of Belonging	0.1
Job Ethic	0.3	Sense of Mission	0
Leading Others	0.1	Sense of Timing	−0.1
Long Range Planning	−0.2	Sensitivity to Others	0.1
Material Possessions	0.4	Status and Recognition Drive	0.3
Meeting Standards	0.3	Surrendering Control	0
Monitoring Others	0.3	Systems Judgement	0.4
Persistence	0.4	Theoretical Problem Solving	0.2
Personal Accountability	0.4	Understanding Attitude	0.1
Personal Commitment	0.4	Understanding Motivational Needs	−0.2
Personal Drive	0.1	Using Common Sense	0.4
Personal Relationships	0.1		

Pearson's correlation coefficient

Correlation	Negative	Positive
Small	−0.3 to −0.1	0.1 to 0.3
Medium	−0.5 to −0.3	0.3 to 0.5
Large	−1.0 to −0.5	0.5 to 1.0

Performance

1   Below Average

2   Average

3   Above Average

4   Excellent

5   Genius

The Seven Genius Patterns (abbreviated)

The Balanced Pattern
Masters: Head, Hand, Heart
Blind spots: None

Pattern Description:

You are very well developed in all three classes of talent (Head, Hand and Heart) and with equal proportion for each. You will be very attentive and competent in all three dimensions from schematic thinking, to practicality to valuing others. You will not develop a blind spot for any on class of talents. You appreciate and possess equal strengths in: systems, rules, structure, concrete organization, detailed planning, and people skills. You are a versatile, quick learner in all of these areas. This can also lead to your becoming easily bored or anxious in positions that require excessive over or under focus on any one dimension to the exclusion of the others (e.g. sales activity that doesn't allow for ample concern for, or connection with, the individual will fail to satisfy your Heart Master thus leaving you unsatisfied by the role).

When reacting subconsciously, your genius motto becomes, "It's important to think about it, and talk about it, and get it done too."

Masters:
- Head, Hand and Heart dimensions
- Versatility in dealing with people, job functions or systems equally
- Quick learning ability in a wide variety of business areas
- Stability, dependability
- Understanding and communicating with others
- Planning and organizing
- Schematic and strategic thinking

Blind Spots:
- Technically you have none—as far as the dimensions are concerned
- You can, however, get easily bored with limited tasks and responsibilities
- May become anxious if all three areas (people, performance and structures) aren't utilized
- Can feel unchallenged if all three areas (i.e. Head, Hand and Heart) are not capitalized in whatever you do

You prefer to get results by: Creating a strategic plan, then taking action while involving others.

The Social Pattern
Masters: Hand, Heart
Blind spots: Head

Pattern Description:

You tend to interpret situations in terms of people and their social and work relationships as well as the practical aspects of what is right in front of you, what must happen now to achieve results or accomplish the task at hand. This can cause you to become blind to or become distracted from the big picture, focusing instead on what others feel and what the immediate situation shows. You can ignore the rules, structure or policies if they do not seem relevant to the situation at hand, favoring to adapt and create whatever new structure or rules fit the current reality at the moment—in order to achieve results. The here-and-now and the productive application of human resources take precedence over structure and organization, or compliance with previously established (what you might consider stale or irrelevant) policies and procedures. The more stressed or faster you go, the greater your dislike for lots of structure. In such situations, you prefer to work freely without lots of controls. In really high velocity you are much too concerned with people and getting things done than being constrained by such things as rules that "don't understand the real-time needs." The more stressed you get, the less time you have to stop and create an elaborate structure or system of steps. You would rather remain open and just improvise, adapt and overcome as the situation calls for it.

When reacting subconsciously, your genius motto becomes, "Don't over think it, just get everyone on board let's go do it."

Masters:
- Teamwork or any group effort
- Interpersonal communication
- Empathy
- Practical thinking
- Understanding others
- Concrete organizing and functional needs

Blind Spots:
- Strong preference for production deadlines or personnel needs in favor of rules, structure or rigid policies
- Staunch guidelines
- Tendency to take an *ad hoc* approach as the situation calls for
- Long Range planning

You prefer to get results by: Acting in the now while involving others.

The Director Pattern
Masters: Head, Heart
Blind spots: Hand

Pattern Description:

You are a person who understands situations in terms of people and the structure within which they exist, or the integration of human resources with an established organization, system, order, or rules and policies. You prefer coordinating or balancing the needs of people and the system that they are a part of (e.g. society, corporate, etc.). You're very good at this. You understand people very well, and enjoy working within a structured and orderly environment or set of processes. You develop a blind spot, however, for the Hand dimension that can cause you to miss the functional or tactical aspects of the situation or task. Things like tangible or practical details, key features, and sense of urgency are examples of things that you can lose sight of. The more stressed you get, the more you want to slow down, isolate one thing at a time and work through it by giving it lots of thought and discussion.

When reacting subconsciously, your genius motto becomes, "Stop to think and talk about it sufficiently before proceeding."

Masters:
- Integrating systems with human resources
- Organizational and human resource management
- Respect for policies
- Understanding people
- Big-picture or schematic thinking

Blind Spots:
- Attention to practical details
- Speed and urgency
- Detailed work, quality control
- Concrete organizing

You prefer to get results by: Creating a strategic plan then achieving those results through others.

The Efficient Pattern
Masters: Head, Hand
Blind spots: Heart

Pattern Description:

You are someone who focuses a lot on the efficiency and results of a situation. You are driven to succeed in whatever endeavor you partake and have very good to excellent ability to see the big picture that must be taken, and the smaller detail which will get you there. Efficient organization and completion of objectives and of the work function in particular, are where you place your attention. Your focus becomes that of, "let's carefully plan the process—then execute," which can, however, leave little room for consideration of the human elements around you. Individual personal needs or values can become your blind spot, causing you to overlook, or not consider sufficiently, the humanistic needs of a situation. While very good at big-picture thinking (planning it) and tactical operations (getting it done), factoring in the human dimension can be something you either don't see as clearly or just forget to consider amid all the planning and executing. The more stressed you get the more you are likely to fixate on creating order out of any chaos, and acting on objectives yourself, and the more likely you are to forget to factor in the thoughts and needs of others as much.

When reacting subconsciously, your genius motto becomes, "Make sure to think it through, but then get it done, no time to talk about it."

Masters:
- Efficient and productive organization and fulfillment of work
- Conceptual thinking
- Conceptual and concrete organizing
- Schematic and or detail oriented thought
- Big-picture thinking

Blind Spots:
- Communication and people skills
- Human awareness
- Balancing people needs with organizational and objective needs

You prefer to get results by: Creating a strategic plan and then acting on it.

The Supportive Pattern
Masters: Heart
Blind spots: Head, Hand

Pattern Description:

   You place a lot of value on people, compared to getting functional objectives done or working within a system of established rules. You really can understand people and communicate with them very well, and when faced with problems you will seek to preserve harmony among people and personal relationships first. Your blind spots can become the strategic big picture and the functional or practical deliverables of the task. Your attention to the humanistic aspects can cause you to lose focus on the procedural or tactical aspects and you can become more focused on preserving relationships and individual needs than with things like the overall plan and action. The more stressed you get, the more you can become blind to the strategic and tactical needs of the situation, focusing almost exclusively on the personal aspects.

When reacting subconsciously, your genius motto becomes, "I need to know how everyone feels before I can decide what needs to be done and how."

Masters:
   • Communication and people skills
   • Generally good in resolving people conflict problems
   • Sensitivity to others
   • Human awareness

Blind Spots:
- Objectivity where people are involved
- Relegating performance and rules compliance behind the personal feelings and needs of people
- Pragmatism
- Schematic thinking

You prefer to get results: Through others.

The Practical Pattern
Masters: Hand
Blind spots: Head, Heart

Pattern Description:

You are, above all else, practical. You understand reality and respond to situations in a very practical way. You do not get overly personal, nor do you tend toward being overly dogmatic to certain rules. In actuality, in stressed situations, you pay much less attention to relationships and rules than may be needed sometimes. The rules that drive you are functional rather than formal or personal. As a result you are much better at implementation, goal achievement and focusing on getting the work done than you are at bigger-picture strategic work or leveraging personal needs or concerns. Due to this you may actually have to be careful not to ignore some rules, or other's opinions, too much. The more stressed you get, the less you look at how something should "ideally" be done, or "who" could get it done, and the more likely you are to just make it happen (typically by yourself).

When reacting subconsciously, your genius motto becomes, "Stop thinking and talking about it…Just Do It!"

Masters:
- Capacity for work, both in terms of the application and operation of machines
- Very much a business mind set versus personal
- Strong practical thinking
- Organizational skills
- Just Do It mentality

Blind Spots:
- Communication with others (especially with superiors and authority figures)
- Likely tends to ignore established guidelines and peoples needs in favor of pragmatic functionality or goal achievement
- Established or rigid policies and procedures

You prefer to get results by: Taking action yourself—quickly most times.

The Systematic Pattern
Masters: Head
Blind spots: Hand, Heart

Pattern Description:

You are someone who interprets situations primarily in logical terms, from a theoretical or rational perspective, rather than an emotional or tactical level. Your focus tends to be on the established rules, policies, or procedures and how they relate to the situation at hand. You prefer to solve problems methodically and possibly through your own "system" for such things. You are much more in favor of order and structure than you are chaos and ambiguity. Having a set way of doing things is very important to you, and you feel that following that order allows you to be the most productive. You are very good at seeing the big picture and planning overall operations or direction. You can become blind, however, to the emotional and practical aspects of the situation. You can miss functional details at the minute level by being focused exclusively on the big picture. The more stressed you get, the more you will retreat into the confines of your own mind choosing to process and consider and plan before acting and eliciting the opinions of others.

When reacting subconsciously, your genius motto becomes, "Stop and Think."

Masters:
- Use of logic
- Long range planning

- Schematic thinking
- Strategic or big-picture thinking

Blind Spots:
- Empathy
- Being practical
- Taking instinctive action quickly
- Performance in vague, highly dynamic, constantly changing or non-defined environments

You prefer to get results by: Creating a system that when followed by others will lead to achieving the objective.

ACKNOWLEDGMENTS

To those who believed in me and sacrificed so much to allow me the time it took to bring this vision to life. To Dr. Robert S. Hartman, the visionary without whom the world would have no way to measure their genius. To our geniuses, Dan, Bill, Frances, Garry, Larry, Marshall, Michael, Randy and Tony, and all the others who gave of their valuable time to share their genius with the rest of the world. To the 300,000 who played no small role in helping to divine the secret to achieving the 5th level of performance.

To all our consultants around the world who help spread that knowledge and benefit. To the Master Mind group, Allan B., Allan M., Barb, Bets, Bill, Bryan, Cathy, Dan, David, Gavin, Gerry, Heather, Jennifer, Jerry, Jim, Kate, Kim, Laura, Renier, Ruth, Scott, Stewart, Sue, Tammy and Walt & Ann, for their objective and sometimes brutally honest feedback that helped ensure that the message of this book was conveyed in a way that allowed it to benefit everyone.

To Jim at Strattomedia for making the outside of the book look great. To the team at 1106 Design for making the inside of the book look equally as great and to David Lombardino for making it enjoyable to read.

To all the board members at the Hartman Institute, past and present, whose belief and perseverance allowed Dr. Hartman's original work to survive and thrive.

Thanks all!

NOTES

Amen, Daniel G. (1998). *Change Your Brain, Change Your Life.* Three Rivers Press: New York.

Andriessen, Daniel. (2004). *Making Sense of Intellectual Capital.* Elsevier, Inc.: Boston.

Angus, Jeff. (2006). *Management by Baseball.* Collins: New York.

Bailey, Simon T. (2008). *Release Your Brilliance.* Collins: New York.

Bennis, Warren and Patricia Ward Biederman. (1997). *Organizing Genius.* Perseus Books: Reading.

Blanchard, Ken, Stephen Covey, James Niblick et al. (2008). *Blueprint for Success.* Insight Publishing: Sevierville.

Bradberry, Travis. (2007). *The Personality Code.* Penguin Group: New York.

Buckingham, Marcus and Curt Coffman. (1999). *First, Break All the Rules.* Simon & Schuster: New York.

Byrum, C. Stephen. (2006). *From the Neck Up: The Recovery and Sustaining of the Human Element in Modern Organizations.* Tapestry Press, Ltd.: Littleton.

Covey, Stephen G. (2004). *The 8th Habit.* Free Press: New York.

Damasio, Antonio R. (1994). *Descartes' Error: Emotion, Reason, and the Human Brain.* Avon Books, Inc.: New York.

Drucker, Peter F. (1965). *The Future of the Industrial Man.* The New American Library: New York and Tokyo, The New English Library Limited: London.

Edwards, Rem B. (2000). *Religious Values and Valuations.* Paidia: Chattanooga.

Gelb, Michael J. (2002). *Discover Your Genius.* HarperCollins Publishers: New York.

Gerber, Michael E. (2001). *The E Myth Revisited.* HarperBusiness: New York.

Gladwell, Malcolm. (2005). *Blink: The Power of Thinking without Thinking.* Little, Brown and Company: New York.

Godin, Seth. (2007). *The Dip.* Penguin Group: New York.

Godin, Seth. (2001). *Unleashing the Ideavirus.* Hyperion: New York.

Goldsmith, Marshall. (2007). *What Got You Here Won't Get You There.* Hyperion: New York.

Goldsmith, Marshall, Laurence Lyons and Alyssa Freas. (2000). *Coaching for Leadership.* Jossey-Bass/Pfeiffer: San Fransisco.

Gregerman, Alan S. (2007). *Surrounded by Geniuses.* Sourcebooks, Inc.: Naperville.

Hartman, Robert S. (1967). *The Structure of Value.* Southern Illinois University Press: Carbondale and Edwardsville.

Hoch, Stephen J., Howard C. Kunreuther and Robert E. Gunther. *Wharton on Making Decisions.* John Wiley & Sons, Inc.: New York.

Klein, Gary. (1998). *Sources of Power*. The MIT Press: Cambridge and London.

Klein, Gary. (2003). *The Power of Intuition*. Doubleday: New York.

Machiavelli, Niccolo. (1965). *The Art of War*. Da Capo Press: Cambridge.

Maltz, Maxwell. (1998). *Zero-resistance Selling*. Prentice Hall: Paramus.

Marr, Bernard. (2005). *Perspectives on Intellectual Capital*. Elsevier Inc.: Boston.

Martin, Linda and David G. Mutchler. (2006). *Fail-Safe Leadership*. Delta Books: Mohnton.

Pomeroy, Leon. (2005). *The New Science of Axiological Psychology*. Rodopi: Amsterdam and New York.

Robbins, Anthony. (1991). *Awaken the Giant Within*. Free Press: New York.

Root-Bernstein, Robert and Michele. (1999). *Sparks of Genius*. Houghton Mifflin Company: New York.

Seligman, Martin E.P. (1990). *Learned Optimism*. Pocket Books: New York.

Smith, Bob. (2004). *Discover Your Blind Spots*. Clear Direction, Inc.: Dallas.

Lao-Tsu. (1993). *Tao Te Ching*. Hackett Publishing Company: Indianapolis.

His Holiness the Dalai Lama. (2005). *The Universe in a Single Atom*. Morgan Road Books: New York.

Thomson, David. (2006). *Blueprint to a Billion*. John Wiley & Sons, Inc.: Hoboken.

Tolle, Eckhart. (2005). *A New Earth*. Penguin Group: New York.

Wilson, Timothy D. (2002). *Strangers to Ourselves*. The Belknap Press of Harvard University Press: Cambridge and London.

INTERVIEWEES

I interviewed a lot of people for this book, but those listed here gave significantly of their time, beliefs, experience and insights—all in the hopes of helping others find their genius. Thanks to all of them for their valuable time and input.

Anthony Robbins

For the past three decades, Anthony Robbins has served as an advisor to leaders around the world. A recognized authority on the psychology of leadership, negotiations, organizational turnaround, and peak performance, he has been honored consistently for his strategic intellect and humanitarian endeavors. He has directly impacted the lives of more than 50 million people from over 100 countries with his best-selling books, public speaking engagements, and live events. Robbins has been honored by Accenture as one of the "Top fifty Business Intellectuals in the World"; by Harvard Business Press as one of the "Top 200 Business Gurus"; by American Express as one of the "Top Six Business Leaders in the World"; by Forbes as a Top 100 Celebrity; by Justice Byron White as one of the world's "Outstanding

Humanitarians"; and by the International Chamber of Commerce as one of the top 10 "Outstanding People of World."

Dan Lyons

Dan Lyons is the Founder and President of Team Concepts, Inc. (1995) and founder of the non-profit Champions of Hope, Inc. (2002). As an oarsman, Dan rowed on seven U.S. National Teams, during that period winning two world bronze medals, a world gold medal, and a Pan American gold medal. In 1988, he competed in the Seoul Olympics in the coxed pair. He has won eleven National Championships in various events. Since 1983 Dan has coached at the U.S. Naval Academy, St. Joseph's Prep in Philadelphia, Oxford University, Stanford University, Drexel University, Georgetown University, and is now an elite coach at Penn Athletic Club in Philadelphia. His remarkable rowing career was recognized in 1997 with his induction into the US Rowing Hall of Fame in Mystic, CT. Dan is the subject of two books (*True Blue,* and *The Yanks at Oxford*) as well as the movie *True Blue* which depicts events during the famous mutiny at Oxford in 1986.

Frances Hesselbein

Frances Hesselbein is the Chairman of the Board of Governors of the Leader to Leader Institute (formerly the Peter F. Drucker Foundation) and its Founding President. Mrs. Hesselbein was awarded the Presidential Medal of Freedom, the United States of America's highest civilian honor, in 1998. The award recognized her leadership as Chief Executive Officer of Girl Scouts of the U.S.A. from 1976–1990, her role as the Founding President of the Peter F. Drucker Foundation, and her service as "a pioneer for women, diversity and inclusion." Her contributions were also recognized by two Presidential Commissions on National and Community Service. She serves on many nonprofit and private sector corporate boards, including the Board of the Mutual of America Life Insurance Company, New York, the American Express Philanthropy, the Boards of the Center for Social Initiative at the Harvard Business School, the Hauser Center for Nonprofit Management at the Kennedy School, and U.C.S.D. Graduate School of

International Relations and Pacific Studies. Mrs. Hesselbein is Editor-in-Chief of the award-winning quarterly journal *Leader to Leader*. She is the author of *Hesselbein on Leadership* and *Be, Know, Do: Leadership the Army Way*, introduced by General Eric K. Shinseki.

Laurence Higgins, MD

Dr. Higgins is an Associate Professor in the Department of Orthopedic Surgery at the Brigham and Women's Hospital and is Board Certified in Orthopedic Surgery. He completed his residency at the Hospital for Special Surgery (HSS) in New York City. He is the Brigham and Women's Hospital Chief, Harvard Shoulder Service as well a Chief of the Sports Medicine and Shoulder Service. He specializes in sports medicine and shoulder injuries. He performs arthroscopic surgery of the shoulder and knee as well as total shoulder replacements.

Dr. Higgins completed a Fellowship in Sports Medicine and Shoulder Surgery at The Center for Sports Medicine at the University of Pittsburgh Medical Center and is the Team Physician for Brookline High School. He has been a Team Physician for Duke University, The University of Pittsburgh Athletic Teams and the professional football team (NFL) the Pittsburgh Steelers.

Marshall Goldsmith

Marshall Goldsmith is one of the world's foremost authorities in helping leaders achieve positive, measurable change in behavior: for themselves, their people, and their teams. Marshall has been ranked in the Wall Street Journal as one of the "Top 10" consultants in the field of executive development. His work has received national recognition from the Institute for Management Studies, the American Management Association, the American Society for Training and Development and the Human Resource Planning Society. Marshall is one of a select few consultants who has been asked to work with over fifty major CEOs. His clients have included corporations, such as: 3M, Accenture, American Express, Boeing, GE, General Mills, Glaxo SmithKline, IBM, Johnson & Johnson, KPMG, McKinsey and Motorola. He has helped to implement leadership development processes that have impacted over one million people. Amazon.com has ranked five of his books as the #1 best sellers in their field.

Michael Lorelli

Mike Lorelli's thirty-year career spans a wide range of consumer products and services, and B2B categories, with responsibilities for both domestic and international units. Dr. John Rutledge, Chairman of Rutledge Capital, said, "I would invade China with Mike alone in a rubber boat." Mike's assignments at PepsiCo included Executive Vice President—Marketing, Sales and R&D for PepsiCo North America, President of PepsiCo East, a $1.5 billion operating company, and President for Pizza Hut's International division where he led a "global or bust" charge, resulting in expanding the company's presence from sixty-eight to ninety-two countries, surpassing McDonalds in country count. During his PepsiCo tenure, he is given credit for authoring the soft drink company's "Big Event Marketing" strategy, which coupled the product with leading-edge events in entertainment, sports, consumer electronics, movies and home video.

Randy Haykin

Randy is an entrepreneur, angel investor and venture capitalist located in the Bay Area. His career spans thirty years in Consumer, Enterprise and Infrastructure businesses in both technology and consumer services areas. In 1995, he founded Interactive Minds, which later became Outlook Ventures, a San Francisco-based software venture capital family of funds. The firm has funded over thirty early-stage technology firms since inception, including: Overture, Wit Captial, Impulse Buy Network, DotBank, eTeamz, Active Networks, eCirlces/Classmates.com, Epicentric, Lasso Logic, Echopass, Loyalty Lab, Xactly, Digital Chocolate, and Reply.com. A member of the Faculty at UC Berkeley's Haas School of Business, Randy teaches the "New Venture Finance" course at the school. As an entrepreneur, Randy was the founding VP Sales & Marketing at Yahoo, Founding COO at Electric Minds and Overture (1997, with IdeaLab). He has been the Director of Business Development at Paramount Technologies and Director/Creator of the Global Multimedia at Apple.

Mickey Rogers

Mickey Rogers is a demolitions expert and is Founder and CEO of Advanced Blasting Services, LLC. (ABS). ABS is a full service drill and blast company that also offers consulting services. Mickey's expertise has been utilized in projects ranging from small rock trenching jobs to marine blasting to the demolition of concrete bridges, steel bridges and smoke stacks. Mickey has personally consulted on and directed the demolition of many successful industrial, commercial and residential projects. He is no stranger to the mining and quarry sector either, having conducted projects throughout the continental U.S.A., Hawaii, and Mexico. Regardless of the type of project or the scope of work, Mickey and ABS strive to perform beyond the client's expectations to obtain the desired end result and he has become a leading expert in his field. With over thirty years of experience Mickey is a recognized leader throughout the blasting industry. His innovative work has been featured in the *Journal of Explosives Engineers* and on the *Discovery Channel*.

Garry Titterton

Garry has been in the advertising world since 1960 so there isn't much he *hasn't* seen. As CEO of D'Arcy Asia Pacific he turned around a loss of $6.5 million U.S.D. to being profitable within two years, and from being outside the "Top 20" in Asia Pacific to the fifth largest agency.

As Executive Vice President McCann Erickson Asia Pacific, Garry lead the Coca-Cola agency team that created a promotion that achieved 40 million entries in Japan and set a *Guinness Book* record for the largest number of respondents to a promotional campaign. As Executive Vice President McCann Erickson Europe he created the first in-house brand and also lead the team that created the "I Can't Believe It's Not Butter" campaign (the first "Brand" to be the subject of an editorial in *The Times* of London). Garry was even part of a three-man team that created *Choix* (a premium chocolate brand later sold to Alders plc).

He has been President of the St. Vincent de Paul Society (a society to alleviate poverty); Governor of Kent Institute of Art & Design (KIAD), and Chairman and Trustee of the KIAD Foundation (the fund raising arm of KIAD). Garry is a lecturer at the Graduate business school based in Fontainebleau at INSEAD in France, and the Madrid University MBA program.

Rosemary Hygate

From the eighteenth birthday party held for her at the House of Lords in England (her godfathers were Lord Monckton of Brenchley and the late Major Alistair Miller of the Scots Guard and Deputy Lieutenant of Oxfordshire) Rosie has been accustomed to being around royalty (of the British or Hollywood kind). Starting out working with her father in London as an executive assistant to the late Sammy Davis Jr. and performing public relations work for other fellow rat-pack members, Rosie has made a career out of public relations and executive assistant work to some of Hollywood's biggest names. At her request, for reasons of anonymity, the names of those she has worked for (still living at least) shall remain confidential, but suffice it to say that her employment record reads like a virtual who's who of movie stardom. As an executive assistant, she has fulfilled duties as varied as managing multiple houses and their staff to coordinating international press junkets and movie premiers. She has helped manage investments in horse farms, restaurants and aircraft and sailing ships—even helped manage a production company.

INDEX

ADDITIONAL RESOURCES

Check out some of the additional resources available to help you discover and unleash your genius.

- **5th Level Performance Workshops:** Learn in a team environment in these live two-day workshops facilitated by one of our certified 5th Level Performance coaches. Take part in additional exercises, benefit from additional measurement tools and receive personal assistance with your role building, future visioning and other activities and exercises to help you reach your 5th level of performance—faster. (*www.whatsyourgenius.com/workshops*)

- **5th Level Coaching:** Work one-on-one with your own private 5th Level Coach. These coaches are experienced executive and life coaches who have met our minimum requirements for education, experience and ability, and are then certified through a rigorous six-month training program to learn how to best help you reach your 5th level of performance. (*www. whatsyourgenius.com/flc*)

- **Corporations:** If you are a corporation that is interested in learning how to unleash the hidden genius within your organization, please contact us at *genius@innermetrix.com* and you will be connected to one of the Certified Innermetrix Consultants who worked on this research and can help you with corporate needs.